Walter J Clutterbuck

About Ceylon and Borneo

Being an Account of Two Visits to Ceylon, one to Borneo

Walter J Clutterbuck

About Ceylon and Borneo
Being an Account of Two Visits to Ceylon, one to Borneo

ISBN/EAN: 9783744798181

Printed in Europe, USA, Canada, Australia, Japan

Cover: Foto ©Andreas Hilbeck / pixelio.de

More available books at **www.hansebooks.com**

ABOUT
CEYLON AND BORNEO

BEING

AN ACCOUNT OF TWO VISITS TO CEYLON, ONE TO
BORNEO, AND HOW WE FELL OUT ON
OUR HOMEWARD JOURNEY

BY

WALTER J. CLUTTERBUCK, F.R.G.S.

AUTHOR OF 'THE SKIPPER IN ARCTIC SEAS'
AND JOINT AUTHOR OF 'THREE IN NORWAY' AND 'B.C. 1887'

WITH FORTY-SEVEN ILLUSTRATIONS
AND TWO MAPS

LONDON
LONGMANS, GREEN, AND CO.
AND NEW YORK: 15 EAST 16th STREET
1891

PRINTED BY
SPOTTISWOODE AND CO., NEW-STREET SQUARE
LONDON

PREFACE

This book is about Ceylon as it was fourteen years ago; about Ceylon as it is now; also about Brunei, which is a very, very ancient part of Borneo; and it treats in a few chapters of North Borneo, which is to all appearances ' a bran new place.'

Everyone sees things from a different point of view. My view may be hopelessly uninteresting to the world in general, but if you have undertaken to scan this book you must put up with it. Yes! read on; feeling sure that something better is coming. Will it come?

CONTENTS

CHAPTER		PAGE
I.	Arrival in Colombo	1
II.	Travelling Up Country	11
III.	The same Journey in 1890	15
IV.	On Tea	26
V.	Coolies	34
VI.	Way Down Upon the Kehelgama River	46
VII.	The Planter's Life	54
VIII.	Down the Dickoya Valley	63
IX.	The 'Bopats'	71
X.	In the Lower Country	82
XI.	Mount Lavinia	88
XII.	Something about the Natives at Mount Lavinia	101
XIII.	Travelling in Ceylon	118
XIV.	At Manly's	124
XV.	Departure from Ceylon	131
XVI.	A Shipload of Emigrants for North Borneo	132
XVII.	Arrival at Sandakan	139
XVIII.	We Start for the Wilds	149

CHAPTER		PAGE
XIX.	IN THE LOW-LYING TOBACCO COUNTRY	155
XX.	BOS BANTENG	159
XXI.	SOME BORNEAN NATIVES	164
XXII.	OUR RETURN	176
XXIII.	NATIVES OF NORTH BORNEO	186
XXIV.	ELEPHANTS	192
XXV.	LABUAN	200
XXVI.	BRUNEI	207
XXVII.	BRUNEI (*continued*)	215
XXVIII.	SINGAPORE	224
XXIX.	WE SET OUT ON OUR RETURN	234
XXX.	ABOARD A M. M. STEAMER	241
XXXI.	WE ARRIVE AT MARSEILLES	250
	APPENDIX	259

LIST OF ILLUSTRATIONS

FULL-PAGE ILLUSTRATIONS

'In Tow' Coming from Muara to Labuan . . *Frontispiece*	
In Peradeniya Gardens . . . . . *To face page*	28
Kondesalle Ferry . . . . ,,	84
Bullocks at Kondesalle . . . . . ,,	89
The Bamboos. From Warleigh Ford, Dickoya ,,	120
Van's Native Servants from Java . . . ,,	193
Native Women at Brunei . . . . ,,	217
A Native Fisherman's Dwelling near Muara ,,	225

ILLUSTRATIONS IN TEXT

	PAGE
A Group of Singhalese Lads beneath the Cocoa-nut Trees	9
Washing Cows in the Lake at Colombo	19
Douglas's Old Bungalow	23
A Tamil Coolie Woman picking Tea	27
Large Tea Leaf. Tea Flower and Seed. The 'Pluck' .	31
Tamil Woman's Earring	40
An Old Tamil Woman covered with Jewellery . .	42
Edward and Douglas inspecting Cattle	55
The Mortared, Whitewashed Lump of Clay. . .	69
The Old Malay Conductor	72
Singhalese Men Washing for Gems	77
The Ants on my Shirt-sleeve	79

	PAGE
THE STICK INSECT	80
THE TROTTING BULLOCK	86
THE SEA COAST	90
MARCH, 1876	91
MARCH, 1877	91
CROWS AT MOUNT LAVINIA	94
ABOUT THIRTY-SIX FEET FROM THE GROUND	97
KATAMARANGS ASHORE	101
'ELP !! 'ELP !!	105
HAIR-CUTTING	108
NEAR MOUNT LAVINIA	114
A BULLOCK HACKERY	129
A CHINAMAN	135
THE PIER AT KUDAT	141
OUR BUNGALOW IN BORNEO	167
THE 'TONGERED'	169
THE BACK OF A DUTCHMAN'S BUNGALOW IN THE LOW COUNTRY ABOUT THIRTY MILES INLAND	179
ANGSEUNA TREES, LABUAN	202
TOWN OF BRUNEI ON PILES	209
A HOUSE IN BRUNEI	211
ALL THAT IS TO BE SEEN OF A BRUNEI BOAT RETIRING	219
THE BRUNEI STREET LAMP	220
BOYS BATHING BENEATH MY BUNK ABOARD THE BORNEO BOAT	228
A CHINAMAN'S RAZOR	231
A CHINAMAN'S BOAT AT SINGAPORE	232
A KATAMARANG AT MOUNT LAVINIA	244

MAPS

SANDAKAN HARBOUR	*to face page* 150
BRITISH NORTH BORNEO AND BRUNEI	*at end*

ABOUT CEYLON AND BORNEO

CHAPTER I

ARRIVAL IN COLOMBO

It was on December 20, 1889, that I arrived at Colombo in Ceylon. I am going to tell you just what I saw in the island on that occasion, and I also wish to give some of my experiences during a short residence there thirteen years previously. There is no use in apology, so let me begin at once.

I stayed with a planter called Douglas two long dry months, and at the end of that time I should not have gone if I had not been turned out. He found that I was not only planted at his up-country bungalow, but that I had become rooted in his house. At length, with one final fell swoop, he dragged me out and I wandered on.

I left, however, behind me some frail tendrils, some fragments of myself, such as a couple of tins of bad tobacco; but as Douglas was not a smoker, he could not be tempted even in a moment of despondency to light a pipe with this. I also left behind me a collarless flannel shirt, and a photograph of Mrs.

Cameron's, representing a young lady in a gauze turban, apparently suffering from sea-sickness, having evidently just remarked that she wished she were dead. There was much pathos in this picture. I also left behind me in my room a smell of smoke, and this was nearly all, if I do not mention Douglas's regrets that I had ever taken it into my head to come out there. Eh! I certainly left all this behind when I quitted Ceylon; was it not enough?

After three weeks of rolling about at sea it seemed strange on arriving at Colombo to find everything still around one, a quiet room on awaking in the morning, instead of the ever-pulsating throb of that never-tiring screw propelling you forward through an apparently ceaseless ocean.

It was strange to lie awake and listen to the shrill crowing of the domestic cock, and Tamil jinrickshaw coolies hallooing to each other from where they stood in the street below in this sort of way—

Whrwwwwww——ah Whrwwwwwww——ah
Whrwwwwwwwwwwwwwwwwww——ah Whrwww ah
Whrwwwwwwwwwwwwwwwwwwww——ah ah!

Then the other fellow—I mean the man who was hallooed to—answered 'Hm,' and presently he would say 'Hm' again. At least this is what their intellectual conversation sounded like to a stranger. Doubtless those who speak the Tamil language fluently would be as much engrossed with the spokesman's tail, as the auditor was outside my bedroom window. Perhaps they would feel inclined to say at the end of each sentence, 'Hm,' just as the Tamil man did who was being talked to in the street.

Then there was the distant hoarse croaking of a hundred crows, with many other sounds which were not the least European, and anything but ship-like. Very soon you began to realise that you were not at sea any longer, and instead of the quiet uneventful life that you had been leading for the last three weeks, you awoke once more to that struggle for existence, that bullying and being bullied, which goes on in our everyday life. Some men are struggling for money, others for health, whilst some are wading on through their span of existence seeking amusement only, and scarcely ever finding it. Of this latter class there were shoals in the hotel at Colombo, as it is the great junction for all travellers who come out eastwards from home.

How delightfully ridiculous some of the fellows in the hotel looked, got up for dinner in the evening with white Eton jackets, white trousers, and gaudy ' cummerbunds ' instead of waistcoats. Certainly they had the advantage of looking cool in this costume compared with the Australians who were hurrying through Ceylon, and who appeared warm, decidedly warm, in their European costumes. The thermometer registered 86° in the shade, and there was enough moisture in the air to stifle one.

Colombo is not a place that inspires Europeans with energy. I agree with the Yankee who said, ' It just slew me to see them fellars sitting there with their stomachs decked out in ribands, and them funny little coats on. Of all the blarmed foolishness that these British colonists are capable of, well, I guess this is the worst.' I am not sure this Yankee was not right in his way of looking at it. It is not as though in Colombo you were in the best hotel in the world, where out of deference to the good feeding you wished to show some respect to the host; but although the dining-room is magnificent and the 'boys' very clean looking, as their appearance and combs were all that one could wish in the way of respectability, still when the hotel was full it was as much as you *could* do to get anything to eat for dinner.

In my opinion the managers might get some tips from the Messageries Maritimes steamers, as without doubt there is some mode by which perfectly tender and well-cooked meat can be provided when alongside the equator, which is at present either unknown or unpractised on shore in equatorial regions.

Talking of dinner reminds me that it is not always beneficial to dine too freely in Ceylon. I was awakened one night in the hotel by hearing a young man in the next balcony to mine soliloquising to the moon; he was saying in a loud and rather husky voice, 'Night, most glorious night, surely thou wert not made for slumber.' Then he began clearing his throat as if he were either going to sing or to cry; I was not sure which. I thought it would be better to stop him, and recommended him to go *straight* to bed, in a rather dictatorial voice, which eventually reduced him to submission. Really it is extraordinary what an effect these Ceylon curries will have upon some folks—whether it is the 'sambal,' or the cocoa-nut, or the onions, I do not know.

The rooms at the hotel are all open at the top to let in air. I do not mean that they are open to the sky, but there is a great space between the rooms and the roof, as the walls only reach part of the way up, and sounds in one room can be heard in another in the most appallingly distinct way.

There was a fellow in the next room to mine who appeared to be suffering from sea-sickness in its most aggravated form. Often he would wake up at midnight, uttering sounds which made one's blood curdle with their hollow gruesomeness. This unfortunate man, I ascertained, had been struck by the sun, and this is the usual way that sunstroke attacks you, besides making you as sick as a dog for some weeks. Amid such horrors of midnight agony, when in the lonesome stillness of tropical darkness the air was suddenly rent by these most sickening sounds, I realised that it is not earth's clear sunshine that always makes folks happy; and, even at the end of a day of most genial brightness, there comes a night which with its long black loneliness seems even darker than our home darkness.

Talking of these low-walled rooms reminds me of a story of two little boys whom I knew. They were staying at the Galle-Face Hotel at Colombo, and a gentleman called Mr. B. and S. was sleeping in the next room. One morning they locked their bedroom door so that no one might come in to disturb them, and getting up on the top of the 'almirah,' or wardrobe, they peered over the ridge of the intercepting wall, and saw Mr. B. and S. trying to shave himself in bed. The situation seemed so comic that they could not help laughing. Mr. B. and S. looked up, and seeing them there said, 'Get away, you naughty boys.' The bigger boy replied, 'Oh, no; please we have come to see you have your bath.' And so they had, poor little dears! and it was a shame to oust them from their seat of vantage.

The hotel at Colombo is a remarkably comfortable house, quite close to the harbour, which it overlooks. It had beautifully clean, well-kept rooms, a mighty verandah; and with its punkahs seemed quite perfection in comparison with the old Galle-Face Hotel which I knew fourteen years ago. The Galle-Face Hotel was formerly managed by a Pārsi,[1] and although it was in those days the best in Colombo, it was nevertheless one of the worst hotels in the great universe. The beds were very hard, the mosquito curtains were holey, and the mosquitoes ravenous. The servants were uncivil, all Christians, and therefore all thieves. I would have recommended visitors to commit some act of violence on their arrival in Colombo—if they had the courage to do it in such an enervating climate—for in the Government prisons food was not so rare, and one's property was protected. As, however, we had arrived unwarned, we had to put up with the mosquitoes in a fleay shake-down.

I remember one day I was staying in that hotel with Douglas—who has always been my bosom friend—and we asked three men to come and lunch with us. We apprised the Pārsi hotel-keeper of this fact early in the morning, in order that he might get a good feed ready for five hungry young men by tiffin time.

When the hour of lunch had arrived we started with inferior soup, and then came some unedibly tough beef-steak. They changed our plates for another course, and we waited awhile full of hope. The champagne was bad and almost undrinkable; however,

[1] This hotel is now under European management, and is exceedingly comfortable and clean.

everyone sipped the nasty wine, and we all became impatient.

We waited longer.

Then we shouted for the servant and told him to make haste with the next course. He left the room and did not return. We called the barkeeper and *besought* him for more food. He looked confused and said there was no more. We were horrified and hungry, while our guests were hungry and amused. We begged that Pārsi on our bended knees to bring us something edible. He replied, 'All right!' as niggers generally do, and in a quarter of an hour six hard poached eggs were placed before us. It seemed impossible to get anything else, and we had to apologise to our guests, who said, 'Oh, don't mention it,' though they must have felt very hungry. We therefore asked them all to dinner at another place. And they remained our friends.

The temperature in Colombo does not vary more than twenty degrees all the year round, and there is a wonderful evenness about the length of the day, only about a quarter of an hour's difference being apparent in the sunrise during summer and winter. You can easily guess what a trying influence this must have upon Europeans, how pale and how washed-out-looking the ladies who reside there become; so that a change home, or at any rate to the hill stations, is necessary every two years.

The folks who live in Colombo, and I believe all dwellers in the East, rise about 5.30 in the morning and have a meal called 'tea,' which is a cup of tea with a slice of toast and jam; then they go straight out for their exercise—either riding or walking—till nine, when they have a bath and sit down to breakfast, which is rather a heavy meal eaten beneath a swinging punkah. They begin with fish and go on to beef-steak, with a course of curry to follow.

The curry in Ceylon is a very different dish to one of the same name in England. Curry here means a course, and a very big course, to itself. You are handed first rice, which is small and exceedingly dry compared with what you generally get at home; then follow three sorts of curry—vegetable, fish, and meat. After this a man comes round with a nasty sort of dried-up fish, called 'Bombay duck,' and a round thin wafer biscuit, which you are intended to pound up in your rice. Lastly, there are two kinds of 'sambal,' which is the heating part of the curry, and which you add to your liking, as the curries are *not hot* in themselves. Point de Galle used to be celebrated for its prawn and oyster curries which were certainly very good; but now the mail steamers come to Colombo, I doubt if Point de Galle is celebrated for anything except its unvarying dulness.

In the hills of Ceylon they make a curry called 'Drum-stick.' This is a vegetable curry composed of the pods of a long thin sort of bean, the shell of which is much too stringy to eat, but the beans and flesh inside the pods are really first-rate. The meat in Ceylon is generally too tough to be good, but you can with safety make your meal off curry and fish, as the fish, although not equal to what you get in Europe, is excellent if well cooked.

The residents of Colombo are engaged in business all through the middle of the day, and they only make a slight lunch or tiffin, saving their appetites for a great dinner at six o'clock. By four business is over for the day, and they enjoy the ocean breezes, either walking or driving along that spray-bedrenched desert, the Galle-Face; a spot which is one's ideal of tropical cheerlessness. With an appetite encouraged by the sea air they return to dinner, which is constructed on exactly the same principles as breakfast.

A GROUP OF SINGHALESE LADS BENEATH THE COCOA-NUT TREES

Then they smoke in a reclining position till bedtime at nine.

The Europeans dress chiefly in white duck. Their costume is complete with a coat, a pair of trousers and a vest. Therefore, dress should not be an expensive item in a man's economy, if it were not for the Singhale dhobi, or washerman, but of him I will say something presently. White duck clothes can be washed continually, but at each washing they shrink a little. Even when a gentleman of Colombo has been fortunate enough to secure a dhobi who will not tear his ducks to pieces in two washings, he finds that when they have been washed several times his costume appears ridiculous to the European eye, for his sleeves retire up his arms and his coat only comes down to his hips.

A few years ago a man was fortunately not judged by his dress in the colonies, as he would be in merry England. A fellow wearing trousers only reaching to his ankles, and a hat that looked as if it might have belonged to his great-great-grandfather, was merely respected as an old colonist, and not regarded as a pawnbroker's assistant, as he might be at home.

CHAPTER II

TRAVELLING UP COUNTRY

How different railway travelling is in Ceylon now to what it was thirteen short years ago! I left Colombo station at 7.30 one morning in December 1889, and arrived at Hatton Station in Dickoya (4,168 feet above sea level) at three o'clock in the afternoon; from thence I had to travel a distance of only five miles along a wonderfully good road before getting to Douglas's bungalow.

Formerly the railway only went to Navalapitiya, which was twenty-nine miles by road from his estate, and we had to get up before cock-crow to catch a train which left Colombo Station at 6 A.M.

I will give my experience of such a journey copied from my journal of March 1877.

It was necessary to take food with you in the train, also to have a meal before starting. We got up at 5 A.M. and sent off our luggage in a bullock cart, a mile and a half to the station. Then we tried to get a little breakfast which had been ordered over-night, but only managed to stow away some tea without milk, and two scraps of toast, for which we were charged two shillings a-head. After this meal we got into a dirty-looking bandy (cab) with a lame horse, and were driven to the station where the train was waiting, as Colombo was the terminus.

The railway line was then badly laid, and you went jolting along at the rate of about twenty miles an hour, in the most distressing fashion. In fact, railway travelling in Ceylon was not then made very fascinating. The luncheon which we brought from the hotel proved a failure, as there were not enough sandwiches, and the claret was very muddy and horribly sour.

The train went slower and slower as we left the low country behind, and the last fifteen miles took an hour and a half to travel over. Navalapitiya was then the terminus, and here every one descended. The platform in those days presented such a picture of jabbering niggers, all anxious to seize and be off with your luggage, that it was necessary to swear and hit at them with your umbrella before you could get them to do as you wished.

Being hot, tired and hungry, we went to the rest-house, or inn. The food was very inferior, and we came to the conclusion that you had to be an experienced colonist in order to relish it. There was only one conveyance to be obtained in the place, and with this we had to content ourselves. The horse was very lame, having something wrong with his *four* legs. He was also exceedingly thin, and looked as though he would not be able to stand up without the carriage to support him.

We had a distance of twenty-seven miles to accomplish before night; in this conveyance we proposed to perform twenty-five miles of it. The owner, who was a Mahommedan Moorman, told us before starting that he had sent on a *fresh* horse for us ten miles in advance, with which to frisk along the second half of the journey.

We therefore started filled up with hope.

First of all a thunderstorm broke over us, with wind and raindrops that seemed as big as shillings; these descended for about an hour, wetting us to the skin, and against which my old mackintosh offered but a pitiful resistance. Then it cleared off for a space, and we walked for a mile or two to help the miserable limping animal.

We caught up our second horse being led by the horsekeeper soon after leaving the rest-house, and it was slowly trotted alongside us until we changed quadrupeds, if you can call them quadrupeds, as they had not four feet to go on. We now sent the first one homewards. I say home*wards*, because it is doubtful whether he was ever able—without the carriage to support him—to stand up during his return journey. I hoped, for the poor horse's sake, that he might fall down dead, and thus get out of this wicked, hard-faring world.

We then advanced at about four miles an hour, as our fresh horse had a very sore shoulder and was appallingly lame. The driver whipped away most mercilessly, making it quite painful to sit behind him. However, the journey had to be accomplished, so we did not remonstrate, but prayed meekly for the end. This wretched horse fell down soon after starting and recut an old broken knee. When we reached Watte Wella rest-house, and sixteen miles of our journey had been completed, he was bleeding both at his knee and at his shoulder.

Here we abandoned our carriage, as we had only

eleven more miles to travel that night. The horse was evidently too feeble to proceed further, without our walking on either side of the shafts and holding him up. We therefore engaged some coolies to carry our lighter luggage, and set out to walk the remainder of our journey to Dickoya. We arrived at our destination about nine o'clock, wet through and rather dispirited. The latter part of our road had been through an elevated district, and Watte Wella rest-house, which was almost our highest point, is 3,628 feet above sea-level.

About thirty years ago all the lower part of Ambegamoua was covered with primeval jungle—and leeches. After that it became very popular with pioneers of coffee-planting, and nearly the whole of the timber was felled and coffee planted in its place. It was found, however, that owing to the great rainfall and the comparative absence of top soil, coffee could not be lucratively cultivated. Many of the estates were therefore abandoned, while others through good management were just kept floating till the time for tea-planting arrived, and then they were once more worked at a profit. Now some of them pay handsomely, others only moderately.

Through this district our road had gradually ascended, winding most picturesquely round the mountain sides and along the valley, in which the scenery was quite beautiful, especially here and there, where one had an extensive view of the lower country, or where one passed through tracts of the original jungle which were then left standing.

CHAPTER III

THE SAME JOURNEY IN 1890

Since my former journey, only thirteen short years ago, the whole of Ceylon had advanced a great many stages in civilisation.

The scenery through which the train took us on the occasion of my second visit was very varied. First of all, on quitting the town of Colombo we came to a country which was very wet under foot. This wetness did not come down from above, at least nothing but the sunshine came down on this day, although in the afternoon the distant horizon looked gloomily black. When I say a 'country wet under foot' I mean a district abounding in paddy-fields, and vegetation all green with tropical luxuriance. Here and there a Singhalese village peeped out full of one-storeyed, partially open-aired, shops called 'caddies.' These had any quantity of plantains hanging from their verandahed tops in clusters, some green and others ripe. Then we saw the schools with their brown cocoa-nut leaved roofs, their wooden pillars, and white mud walls not more than two feet high. Little Singhalese boys looked out from between the posts at the train passing, and stared with their great brown eyes as though they had never seen such a thing before.

We passed Singhalese men and women hacking up the few dried rice-fields with 'mometies.' In Ceylon the spade is unknown; indeed, it would be useless, for the natives never wear boots, and therefore could not tread on the spade as our English labourers do. A momety is a sort of large-bladed hoe, with which all the digging is done. They momety up their paddy-fields instead of ploughing them, because the rice-fields of the valleys are as a rule too small to plough.

We saw clusters of Singhalese dressed in their best white 'comboys' and pink jackets, carrying umbrellas, evidently going to or returning from the nearest town. They looked very pleasing in the distance, as they trooped on beneath beautiful flamboyant trees which overshadowed their pathway, while others walked in gaily coloured troops in the bright sunshine. Then there were old men with perfectly bare shaven faces and heads, dressed in yellow robes, who, I believe, were Buddhist priests, and whom I respected in a mild way.

In the scorched-up rice-fields were numbers of tamed wild buffaloes with ever flopping ears.

The buffalo is unlike the ordinary cow—indeed, rather more unlike than the dog is unlike the cat. The head of the buffalo is more pointed than that of the cow, and it is built on utterly different principles. Its long, thin, ribbed horns slope back on its head, and when the head is lifted into the air the horns come beneath the crest on its neck. It has no hump on its back, as all the cows and oxen out here have. But it has about one hundred and sixteen thick, up-standing, black hairs on its neck, just where a horse's mane would come, and not another hair on its dark coloured body. It even appeared to eat in a different way to the ordinary cow of commerce. You hear none of that chumping sound which makes your heart glad and brings a feeling of content over your spirit in the meadows of England, but there is a sort of wild dash about these brutes which the lover of cows cannot admire.

The buffalo is an essentially water-loving animal. It likes to stand for hours together in the water, with nothing but its head in the air. I saw one which had scraped a sort of nest for itself in the mud of a shallow stream. It was apparently quite contented and happy, sitting and chewing the solacing cud of contentment, with nothing above the brook's surface but its nose, eyes, mouth and horns.

There are three other sorts of cattle which one frequently sees here. The beautiful Indian bullock, with its long thin horns and cream-coloured body, which draws the folks to church at the rate of two and a half miles an hour. It *is* said to trot wonderfully fast, but *I* have never had the advantage of seeing these docile animals summon up the courage to break into a trot.

Then there is the ordinary bullock, which draws carts in this country, and is very slow and stupid. Thirdly, the little black-coloured bullock, which really does go fast in the little 'hackery' for a short distance, and then comes to a full stop. He has reins made of thick string which run through his nose from nostril to nostril, as this, I believe, is the tenderest and most sensitive part of his body. He will run—for one can scarcely call it trotting—for about five miles. Then the hirer of the public hackery has to creep out and get into another, which, with a fresh bullock, is waiting to take him on. Thus he proceeds at the rate of about five or six miles an hour.

Besides the string, which answers as a rein, they have absolutely no harness. The cross piece of wood attached to the shafts which goes over their necks comes in contact with the hump on their shoulders when they are drawing; and they throw back their heads and catch this cross piece just behind their little ears when they go down hill. Thus a bullock is harnessed very differently to a horse, and uses utterly different members in drawing forward or pushing backward. They are very patient, and ready to put up with almost any brutality from man. In fact, they seem to say, in a mute way, 'We will stand anything on earth, but do not twist our tails in that unnatural manner.'

As the train goes up the mountain side, one leaves the low country behind and proceeds at a very slow pace, not only because the ascent is steep, but because it is a Government railway. The scene is wonderfully pretty as you look down over the innumerable green-terraced paddy-fields, interspersed with thick jungle trees topped by the cocoa-nut and areca palms. Away in the distance there stands forth a peaked hill-top, the rocky eminence of which looks like an ancient and almost ruined tower. From its summit our train must appear like a creeping caterpillar feeling its way up amidst the distant rocks and trees, winding its course in and out of the steep hill-side—hill-sides which, in addition to the steaming paddy-fields down below, and the multitudinous tree-tops, with the dark, dark green of the old leaves, and the reddy brown of the young ones, are enlivened here and there with native mud huts nestling in the grassy mountain ridges. The sides of these abodes seemed all split and bursting open from the heat of the sun.

Soon our train reached a station called 'Kaduganawa,' which was just a picture, a most beautiful picture, with pots of luxuriant maiden-hair ferns

WASHING COWS IN THE LAKE AT COLOMBO

rising up in tiers, and clusters of creepers hanging down from the overlapping verandah roof. There was also a very beautiful feathery fern which had the name of *Sellaginda lævigata* on it, displaying palmy leaves all round an earthenware pot suspended from the roof. Then the rest of the station-house disappeared under a mass of pink convolvuli.

There were plantains by the score with their closely packed green fruit, from the centre of which there came out a wiry tail, topped with a sombre, pointed knob. In this hot, damp climate plants will grow where you would think there would not be even space to cling. What beautiful green ferns find a root-hold in the granite rocks along the railway, and seem to sprout as if they were growing in the most luxurious, deep-soiled bank! Wherever a crack opens wide enough to let in a clinging root, you will find the slab covered with ferny creepers.

After leaving all these hot native plantations and rice-fields behind, we got up to where there was a great extent of apparently worn-out land, and where the soil was covered with what appeared to be short brown grass, interspersed with valleys of jungle trees. The nearer hills were in the glare of the sun, while in the distance there were jungle-covered mountains, appearing a deep blue beneath the clouds which hovered over them.

Oddly enough I could not get a carriage when leaving the station at Hatton, as there had been so many folks coming up on this Sunday from Colombo, and so much running about the country, that all the bandies were away from Hatton wandering over the districts of Dickoya and Maskeliya and far up the mountain sides. However, having made friends with the nigger at the station, who was selling most unwholesome-looking cakes and dispensing tea to the hungry travellers, I ventured on two of these cakes, which, though tasting most discouraging, I managed to exist on for many hours.

Then I took my luggage across to the rest-house, where there was a single young man standing in the verandah smoking a cigarette, and looking most insufferably bored, as though he did not care one solitary damn for anything in this world or the next. Before him was a pair-horsed bandy with one dejected-looking horse harnessed to it, and apparently unwilling to move, although it was not guarded by anyone. It kept switching its tail backwards and forwards in the sunshine, as though wishing for nothing so much as to remain there through a never-ending train of hot summer days, till the bandy, which looked as if it would fall to pieces, should become scorched up by the burning rays of that tropical orb, and should moulder away.

I asked this young man why he stood there in contemplative misery, and what he was waiting for. He told me he had come over from Maskeliya, a distance of eighteen miles, to meet his brother, who had arrived upon these spicy shores from England, and was to have left Colombo that day. 'But,' said he, ' as he has not come by this train, and there is no other till to-morrow afternoon at the same hour, I shall not wait any longer, but go back to Adam's Peak, beneath whose shade I will linger out my existence, careless of what becomes of him.' My Maskeliya friend was evidently annoyed, for he added, ' It is too bad when you find that the fellow has not taken the slightest notice of the letter which you wrote him, but is casually drinking the soda-water of Colombo' (not unmixed with English cognac,' he added, sotto voce), ' regardless of your dejection up here amidst these valleys of tea and trouble.'

He was going three miles of his return journey in the same direction that I was, and I asked him for a lift. When he had had the other horse attached to the ramshackle bandy, we got in together, and jingled our way along the hard high road. I had a distance of about eight miles to go altogether before finally arriving at the house whither I was bound. Having been rattled along the road, in and out of the many bends which make a straight path in this mountainous country, we arrived at Wannarajah Bridge, the junction at which my road diverged from that of Maskeliya. Here I got out to walk the two and a half miles to Castlereagh, where I met Douglas waiting for me with two horses and any quantity of baggage-carrying coolies. From thence we rode on a few miles to Claverton bungalow, where I was at home.

Claverton bungalow is quite different from what it used to be when I was here in the time of coffee-planting. It is built much higher up the hillside, and in a more airy position than in olden days.

Then, Claverton was a three-roomed mud hut, placed in the middle of the coffee, whereas now it is a twelve-roomed wooden house, standing in a rose-besprinkled grassy garden, with tall bamboos rising up behind, and great trees with seats beneath their shade on the well-kept sunny lawn. It is in a country far away from factory chimneys and the smoke of coal, where no sound is borne to the ear except the occasional call of coolies, and the splash, splash of the ever working water-wheel. Every now and again a gust of wind blows up the sound of the distant rushing river as it dashes in breakers over its rocky floor.

How different was the scene to which I awoke next morning, when all nature was steeped in glorious sunshine, when the hills looked so cloudless and near, and the far-off mountains, with a white haze rising up from the valley, appeared so distinct, and yet so blue; how different indeed to the misty coldness of a December day in our fog-bedaubed little island! It was now December 23, and about the most beautiful time of the year in Ceylon. The thermometer at this elevation registered 76° in the shade, but in the bright sunshine woe betide the man who ventures forth

DOUGLAS'S OLD BUNGALOW

without first bedecking his head with a 'topee,' or solar hat, as, within seven degrees of the equator, the sun shines as though its rays were perdition let loose.

Douglas's bungalow *used* to be, like all the houses in Dickoya, a mere cottage built of mud, with three rooms twelve feet square, and having a porch or verandah of about the same dimensions before the front door. The roof was made of wooden shingles, split from trees on the estate. The walls which faced the south-west were protected on the outside by weather-boarding, lest the wind and rain should wash them down during the wet season. In spite of this a fall did once occur.

We were awoke at midnight during the tempest which heralds in the breaking of the south-west monsoon, and takes place about May 20, by hearing a most tremendous crash. When we had scrambled out of bed and rushed from our rooms to see what was the matter, we found poor Douglas on the floor, beneath a heap of fallen débris. It was a pitiful sight to watch our recumbent friend trying to extricate himself from his uncomfortable position; whilst the wind and rain, which formerly were kept at bay by the thick wall, were now sweeping through the three-sided bedroom, covering the floor with mud.

Fortunately we were in a glorious colony, where the stormy winds are warm, and where the 'talipot' leaf can be procured in its crispest perfection, so that such accidents were only laughed at by the planters. Having extricated the muddy Douglas, we made up a bed for him in our third, or dining, room, where he slept out the night, and the breach was soon repaired.

The walls of this edifice were altogether in a very shaky condition, and let in the air through many a crack and fissure. It had then been built about four years, and was never intended for a permanent structure.

In this small building three of us lived, and if a couple of visitors turned up—which occurred about every other day—they had to sleep on couches in the dining-room. The servants always slept in the verandah, or on the kitchen floor. This kitchen was a kind of 'lean-to' shed against the back of the house, and was amply supplied with ventilation.

We papered the walls of our dining-room with pictures from the 'Graphic' and 'Illustrated London News,' to keep them from falling in. The result was so fascinating that it was almost impossible to pay attention to anything else when at table in that room. Strangers especially seemed quite carried away by the stirring scenes represented on our walls. Sometimes neighbours who dropped in to breakfast or dinner forgot all about the meal that was going on, and became quite absorbed in some picture of their far-off home, or, indeed, moved to tears by a representation of Queen Victoria distributing Christmas presents to the poor at Osborne. And the steaming fragrance of the bubbling stew scarce recalled their wandering spirits to life and hunger.

Even in Ceylon, art will cast her influence over savage man!

CHAPTER IV

ON TEA

The valley of Dickoya was now wholly occupied by tea plantations, and the jungle that clothed it twenty-eight years ago had almost entirely disappeared. Journeying up the undulating valley from Hatton towards Bogawantalawa, no one can fail to be struck by the way in which the whole surface of the land seems to be green with tea.

The dogged determination and persevering energy of the Englishman have nowhere been more strikingly illustrated than in this country, where only a few short years ago the planters' hopes rested on coffee, and the mountains now so green with tea were then luxuriant with coffee bushes. This product, in which so many millions of English capital were invested, suddenly failed owing to the appearance of an insidious, and so far apparently incurable, disease known as 'Hemileia vastatrix.' With the failure of coffee the hopes of the planter seemed doomed, and a period of depression and disaster naturally followed.

After this cinchona was tried, from the bark of which quinine is made. This threw a transient gleam of hope over the planter's path; but it also proved delusive, as the quantities of bark thrown on the

London market soon reduced the price so much that its production did not continue to pay.

Happily for Ceylon, tea was thought of, and the land which was formerly so prosperous in coffee

A TAMIL COOLIE WOMAN PICKING TEA

promises to be even more prosperous in tea. To convert the ruined coffee estates into tea gardens meant further capital expenditure, and was of course the work of some years. The planters' energy may be gauged by the fact that eight short years ago the main staple of the country was coffee, a wholly topsoil feeder. This has now been changed to tea, which subsists chiefly on subsoil, and Ceylon promises to become before long one of the main factors in the tea markets of the world.

At first the tea was despised, but, having lived down all evil report, it is now admittedly the best tea put on the London market, and commands the highest price. It is very different from the old China teas we used to drink in days gone by.

The recipe for making Ceylon tea is very simple. Put half as much in the pot as you used to put when using China and Japan teas. Pour *boiling* water on it, and let it stand *one* minute only before pouring it out, otherwise it becomes too strong.

The tea plant is what I went out to Ceylon to see. This plant engrosses the whole attention of hundreds of Englishmen; engrosses their attention so much that they cannot think of anything else. They do not talk of anything else, and do not realise that there is anything in this world but tea.

If you look over the whole valley of Dickoya, which is about twenty miles long and four miles broad, you see nothing but tea plantations covering the whole extent. The estates average about 250 acres, and as, when you go out walking or driving, you see little else and hear nothing but tea talked about, the conversation naturally becomes hopelessly tedious to a fellow just come from home.

Some untravelled Englishman may ask, What is this tea plant like? To the casual observer it is exactly like a coffee plant, which I will first endeavour to describe. The leaves and berries somewhat re-

IN PERADENIYA GARDENS

semble the Portugal laurel; it is topped at three feet six inches in height, and it has a single stem which makes a first-rate walking stick. From this stem come a great many nearly horizontal branches, the bearers of the leaves, flowers, and berries. When one comes to regard the *tea* bush closely, it is utterly different, being a real bush, and having a great many stems instead of one. The leaves are of a much deader-coloured green than coffee leaves, with little or no shine on their surface, and they are all, as in the photograph, jagged round the edges. Tea bushes have leaves which vary in size; this depends chiefly on the jart, what we know as Chinese jarts being small, and the Indian being infinitely larger. The large leaf in my photograph was one of an indigenous bush, and next it come the tea seed-pod, the flower, and then the leaves as they are picked for making into tea.

The coolies break off the newly-grown shoots when two leaves have flushed out and another one is coming on, so that in tea drinking we imbibe almost as much juice brewed from the stem as from the leaf. In the photograph I have put on the right-hand side the quantity of leaf and stem plucked together. The stalk is rolled and dried with the leaves, and assists greatly in the composition of tea, being quite as young and soft as they are. After the young green leaves have been picked, they are spread out on 'jute hessian,' called 'tea tats,' in an upper storey of the tea factory, to wither. This withering takes an uncertain number of hours to accomplish, as it makes a great deal of difference whether the weather is fine or not, and from which quarter the wind comes; the wither not being so rapid in wet weather. The leaves are then brought down into the bottom floor of the factory, where they are put into a silently-working machine, and rolled for forty-five minutes. They are next taken to a breaking and sifting machine, where they must be well broken and sifted, judging from the jerky way in which this machine works. The leaves which do not pass through the holes in the bottom of the sifter are now put back into the rolling machine again, where they receive forty-five more minutes of crushing and rolling; this second time they suffer under extreme pressure. When the leaves come out they are all heaped together on a table covered with a cloth, and left there to ferment, which process should take place in about three hours.

What fermentation is I do not know, what the use of it may be I cannot tell; but this I do know, for I have been informed by the best authority in Ceylon, that if the tea is fermented too long it becomes *soft*. I was told this in such a matter-of-fact way that I naturally concluded that everyone except myself knew what soft tea felt like, looked like, and tasted like. I am bound to confess the truth that I personally have not the faintest conception how soft tea *does* taste. English ladies are supposed to know more about tea than anyone else on the face of our globe, and I will leave it to them, therefore, to decide which it is the worse to be compelled to drink, very hard or very soft teas.

When the teas have been fermented, they are put into a tea-drier. There are a great many different sorts of tea-driers; every planter at whose house I stayed told me that, having seen or tried a lot of these machines, he had come to the definite conclusion that his was the only tea-drier worth a cent. He hinted that all other planters were going to the wall as fast as they possibly could, simply because they would use Jamison's down-draught Morocco tea-drier, or some other one that was not exactly the same as his own. When the tea comes out of the drier it is sifted, the

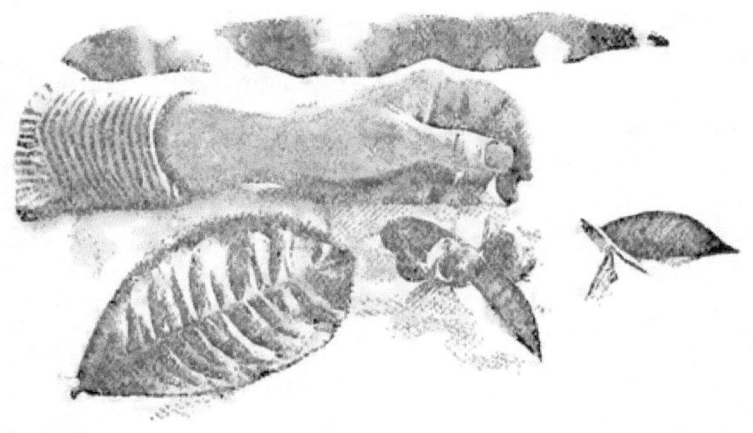

LARGE TEA LEAF   TEA FLOWER AND SEED   THE 'PLUCK'

The lady's hand shows the size of the leaves

finest being Broken Pekoe, the coarser Pekoe, and so on; it is then ready to be packed and sent home. The finer tea, which is generally made from the smaller leaves and stalk only, has infinitely the best flavour.

You can always tell tea leaves from any others with which your grocer may think it cheaper to adulterate the tea, because tea leaves have a jagged exterior—as in the photograph—and other leaves, though they can be rolled up in the same way, still lack those saw-like edges.

Everyone who came to see my friend Douglas was taken straight down to the old coffee store, which had been converted into a tea factory. The smell of crushed tea leaves which arose from the building was quite delicious to anyone visiting the factory for the first time. When we arrived there, this fragrant aroma was wafted to us on the lazy air. Outside the factory was a large water-wheel humming placidly, as the water kept shooting over it with a regular splash, splash. This sound is quieting and gentle in an age of new-fangled turbines and motors, reminding one of a time which is past and gone for ever. It recalls to one's mind all sorts of things connected with trout streams and alders, bluebells and shadows, house flies and *wasps*. When you got inside the factory there were a great many silently-working machines, and beyond was a room two sides of which were covered with canvas, to prevent dust coming in from the main building. In this room a kettle full of water was kept constantly boiling over a lamp made on purpose, and with it the planter continually made cups of tea. When it had stood in the pot exactly five minutes, he poured it out into a white china cup, without a handle, in order to taste it, to look at its colour, and see in cooling how much scum collected on the top. With these teas they rinse out their mouths, not as if they liked them, but simply to taste and distinguish between the flavours. When they have looked wise over it for a moment or two, they eject the rank liquid.

I defy anyone who has not been brought up to

tea-tasting to be able to discover any difference between them, as, by the time he has got to the third cup, his palate has become so confused that although he thinks it necessary to look knowing over fourteen or fifteen cups, really he does not know if he is tasting dust from the bins or Broken Pekoe.

A fellow came down to the factory one day, who did not think we knew how tea should be manufactured. He was a remarkably silent man by nature, and when we took him into the nice clean factory he was evidently surprised, comparing it in his mind with other stores that he had seen, perhaps with his own. Presently we asked him if he would care to taste any of our teas. When he had taken about ten mouthfuls and had ejected them again, he looked satiated. We asked him what he thought of them. First of all he considered for a minute, then he sniffed at the tea leaves from which this very strong brown liquid had been produced, and having extracted all the scent that he could collect, he began fingering them over, one by one, in the light. Presently, after some moments' silent thought, he remarked, 'H'm, pretty good!' and this was all we could get out of him.

It is curious how little satisfies some people. Douglas said to me afterwards, 'Wonderful man, Mount, ain't he?' I naturally wanted to know why. Douglas replied, 'Well, you see, he knows all about *tea*.' It is a remarkable fact that Douglas was as pleased as Punch at this man's visit to the factory.

CHAPTER V

COOLIES

The tea is picked by coolie men and women. Here and there you see a Kangani, or head man, with a stick in his hand watching; and a conductor who is over them all. Our conductor was a rare old sort; he was a Malay by birth, whose parents had come over from Sumatra. I should say that he had been remarkably well instructed in his school days, as he spoke Malay, of course; he knew English, and could swear in Tamil and Singhalese. He had been working on this and the adjoining estate for twenty-six years, so that he could now reckon exactly what time of day his master was likely to come out, and what language he would in all probability use when he lost his temper over the coolies. He knew when he could get away from the men working in the field without his absence being detected. He knew just what he ought to say and leave unsaid when his master was so much annoyed that he could scarcely contain his fury, and was boiling over with rage which almost amounted to despair, in order to turn all the fury off his own back and turn it on to the backs of the Kanganis. Oh, he was a faithful servant, and a true one!

Remark the Tamil coolie sharpening an axe on a bit of granite. He does it as though the axe only wanted scraping for half an hour on any kind of stone, and might be held in various positions during that half-hour, and still at the end of the time would be so sharp as to be capable of cleaving great blocks of wood. Look at him while he is performing this fraud; he works away as if he were doing the cleverest thing under the sun, as if he knew exactly how the axe should be held, and was perfectly master of the situation, till at last you begin to think you know absolutely nothing about sharpening an axe. If you simply regarded this coolie from a distance, it certainly would be borne to your mind that he had got that axe as keen as a razor, and that it only wanted a little stropping before it would be fit for you to shave yourself with. Now step up and try to cut a piece of turnip with the axe, and you find that all this half-hour's labour has been in vain, that in all probability he has been rubbing that tool on a bit of quartz, the result being that it is if possible rather more blunt and jagged than it was before he began.

Then examine the weapon and see how loosely the axe-head is fastened to the long thin stick which he calls the handle, and you no longer wonder that the Tamil man is not very apt at chopping sticks. But mind, this refers only to the Madras Tamil, as the natives of Ceylon are singularly clever with an axe. In fact, they are good at four branches of industry. They can fell jungle really beautifully; you would think to watch them with their long-handled axes that they must have picked up the art of swinging them before they were born, as they never seem to strike a tree an eighth of an inch out.

As domestic servants the Singhalese are wonderfully clever; as washermen they will beat any other nation in beating your clothes to rags; and as bullock-drivers their natural cruelty is unsurpassed in the annals of this world. This is all they *can* do, as far as my experience goes, whereas the Tamil man can be taught to do anything under the sun indifferently, and some few things well. The Tamil certainly is a very good fellow; but all Singhalese are naturally deceitful, and it is only when they have a very strict master or mistress over them that they will work satisfactorily.

It is wonderful how much English is spoken by the Singhalese, the Tamils, and the Moormen in Ceylon. I am told that the most important item in a boy's education is English. Not only can a boy speak English fluently, but he can read and write it.

This was written up in one of the Christian 'Swamy' houses on the adjoining estate, 'God may bless Mr. Alane.' Here the English-speaking Kangani had evidently got the English ever so slightly confused in his brain, as doubtless he intended to put, 'May God bless Mr. Alane.' It was unfortunate this mistake was made, as in another *very* English handwriting beneath this was written simply the words '*He may*!' thus throwing a terrible doubt over the situation.

The Tamil coolie and the Chetti are black spots on this earth, over whom I will linger for the next page or two.

The Tamil coolie is nearly black compared with the Singhalese. He has naturally long black hair, not crisp and curly like that of a negro, but smooth, well-oiled tresses, which he ties up in a knot behind. From his forehead a shaven patch goes back about half-way over his head, and it is from this bald patch that the Tamil coolie's long black hair begins.

They used to shave with glass, but in these days razors are so cheap that in all the native caddies there are men who ply a trade in shaving the Kanganis' heads. However, if you go to the 'lines,' or native dwellings upon an estate, you may see the coolie being shaved in all his native ignorance. It is done in the following way. They break an old black glass bottle and shave each other's heads and faces with the broken fragments, without using soap. This does not as a rule produce a brilliant shave, although it is a very conscientious one.

I think that the Tamil coolie has not an unusual growth on his chin, as it is much less than that of an average European, so that shaving the chin, which takes place about once a week, is not hard work. But there must be a good deal to take off the head, as the hair grows unceasingly there through incalculable ages. Even the most aged and decrepit have hair on their heads which would actually shock our too susceptible old minds. In fact, I am not sure that it does not disgust us to see the aged native meandering along the roads with such perfect hair and teeth.

Ceylon for the ordinary Tamil is now a remarkably healthy and money-making country. In wandering up the Dickoya roads, or through the native shops, you will, in all probability, never meet a beggar, and you rarely see one on whom disease has laid its hold. This is in Dickoya, as I do not know anything about other districts. All the Tamils appear to be hard-working and well fed; their thin legs look as though they had come out of the tempestuous storms of life, away from the disquiet of overpeopled India, to the respectable luxury of rice at six shillings and sixpence a bushel, and high wages in Ceylon (about sixpence a day).

There are three things which a Tamil man fears more than anything else in the world—viz., getting his head wet, the wild elephant, and walking alone near the jungle at night, when our friend might meet 'Pisāsi' (the devil). This latter no Tamil man has been known to do willingly. The Tamil woman, on the contrary, when she goes forth in the rain, puts nothing over her head but the thin cloth she wears about her person. Even in the middle of the day, when the sun is shining blistering hot, as the Yankees would say, she exposes her bare head to its rays without apparently feeling it in the least.

The coolie always wears on the top of his head—mind you, on the *top*, so that it can be no protection from sunstroke—a thick turban, which is often made of an old Turkish cap, surrounded with two or three bright-coloured handkerchiefs. Then, on working days, in the early morning, he decks his body with a very old coat, which once, in years gone by, belonged to a British soldier or policeman, and has been handed down till it has lost all its colour and buttons. The pockets also are worn very threadbare, and are a sort of dirty white, the result of having the hand constantly thrust into them during long years of toilsome labour in other foreign lands. The coat has at length found its way here to be a covering for the Tamil coolie's back. It is merely used as an overcoat, for when the sun gets up it is discarded, and he works with nothing on him but what is called a 'cloth,' which means a long piece of once white linen that has now become a nondescript colour. This covers the middle of his person only, his legs and body being all bare, and showing nothing but brown skin.

The religion of the coolies is Buddhism, and on every estate there is a Swamy house, with a couple of clay images decked in all sorts of old bits of finery, which I am told they worship. I should think these images represent the devil; of this, however, I am not sure, as, oddly enough, I have never seen him. These Swamy huts are small, clay, two-roomed constructions, with the most grotesquely painted mud walls, a mud floor, and thatched roofs.

I went one day to the 'lines' on the estate. The rooms were all close to one another. It is all very well for the planter to have good roomy lines put up for his coolies, but they infinitely prefer living in small, clay-lined, chimneyless rooms, where they can have a fire and make them as close and smoky as possible. When the atmosphere is so thick that you can cut it with a knife, they breathe it in with the utmost gusto. They actually seem to like having bloodshot eyes, the result of a smoky atmosphere.

In these stuffy little habitations they live, and live well. Their food consists chiefly of rice and curry made from vegetables. They never eat meat, except on very grand occasions, when twenty of them kill a pig and devour his flesh.

As we approached the lines there were rather offensive smells, but when we got inside they were wonderfully clean, considering all the floors were strewn with dry cow-dung. It was a Sunday, so a fire burned in nearly all these abodes, and three or four naked much-bejewelled children seemed to inhabit each one. The coolies carry all their worldly wealth on themselves, their wives and children.

Furniture is an unknown commodity with the Tamil coolie, and if he left anything really worth having in his doorless lines, it would in all probability be stolen. He has to put all his gold and silver about the persons of himself and his family, which accounts for resplendency of many of their ears, noses, necks, arms, wrists, ankles and toes.

The ears of female children are cut and leaden rings inserted in the aperture, in order that, when they are grown up, they may have a sort of solid wooden cart-wheel, about two and a half inches in diameter, put in the ear. Some of the women insert any quantity of jewellery in place of this cart-wheel, probably because they happen to be well-to-do, and having already bandaged up their arms, wrists, and noses with ornaments, there is nowhere else to put the superfluity of their wealth.

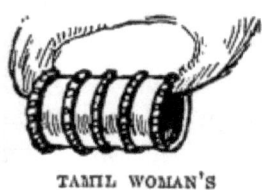

TAMIL WOMAN'S EARRING

The older women wear golden rings in their ears, as you see in the picture. They are about an inch and a half long, and made of the same lustrous material, which is intended to look to us men the most attractive thing under the sun. The Tamil lady who has had two or three husbands, all of whom have been more or less wealthy, has her ears entirely covered with rings and jewellery. My photograph does not show it distinctly, but this old lady had about eight rings in each ear, all of curious savage workmanship, which she no doubt thought very beautiful. How they can sleep with all this jewellery hanging down just where they lay their heads I cannot imagine.

A Kangani's wife decks herself with a heavy mass of plain rounded silver about an inch broad; this she puts on her arm just above the *elbow*, and three or four other bracelets on her wrists, made of silver wallavie and gum. Some of the women have four or five of these wallavie bracelets on each arm, whilst many of their fingers are literally clogged with silver rings.

I saw a woman one day with an enormous cat's-eye set in gold ornamenting her nose. It seems a pity that some of our English women do not adopt this plan of displaying their diamonds. Without doubt they show off to better advantage when placed conspicuously on the nasal organ than if simply worn in rings or bracelets. Who can help seeing them? A mere glance will show the finery with which such a woman is graced! Even a plain woman looks well when adorned with this sort of appendage, as it shows *real earthly value*. They cannot have such jewels stolen, as they are welded into the nose. These ladies seem to think that mental beauty is a mere nothing in comparison with this gilded magnificence.

The merry little children had enormous 'tummies,' the result of living perpetually on quantities of rice; their ornaments were apparently of gold and silver, and were worn round their ankles and necks, I presume for decency's sake, as beyond these they had no covering whatever; but I am forgetting—some of them had silver rings on their toes, so they were not what you can actually call naked.

The coolie's pay of sixpence a day is so enormous that he can afford to dress his children in this astonishing way. Most of the coolies do not care to work more than five days in the week, as they can earn enough riches in that time to support a whole family.

AN OLD TAMIL WOMAN COVERED WITH JEWELLERY

These men also bedeck their persons with jewellery of some kind. I will tell you what a full grown Kangani generally wears. He has a bracelet on his left leg, a ring on his second right toe, four bejewelled earrings in one ear, whilst another gold earring full of jewels hangs from a second puncture higher up on his left ear.

There is one sort of black man in Ceylon who has caused me considerable diversion. This is the 'Chetti.'

In days gone by, before there was a railway up to the tea districts, we had no means of getting money except from the Chetti. I will try to describe this species of nigger as I constantly saw him then. Even now I often wish for his loanly hand to help me on my way, as he was the man from whom we always borrowed small sums of money, and although we had to pay a high rate of interest, it was the only way, in those dark days, of getting money at a moment's notice.

I do not think the Chetties ever wear jewellery; they are a tall race of Indians, and have long smooth-cut features; they shave every hair off their heads and faces. The Chetti creeps round your bungalow enveloped in a long flowing cloak of white linen, which is thrown over his shoulder, and he wears a kind of white hood over his head.

I speak now of a day when we were always 'hard up,' and a Rs. 10 note was a perfect mint of Godsends to us. I speak of a day when we owed the Chetti rupees which ran into three noughts. Never repeat this to the Chetti, but, truth to tell, we could not have paid him even if we had wanted to—but we did *not* want to.

As you sat writing your letters beside the bungalow window, where the mid-day sun came streaming in with an awful heat, suddenly you felt that an eye was fixed on you, and looking up you encountered the dark, glowering gaze of the Chetti demanding to be paid. Or you might go out into your garden, to pull up some weeds and pick the vegetable-marrow which your soul had been doting on for days. But lo! when you took it between your fingers it felt light; presently you saw that it was, like most other things in this land of tropical vegetation and rapid growths, 'rotten to the core,' and you glanced up in displeasure, only to see a silent form gliding from behind a corner of the bungalow. This was Mr. Nana Ramen Chetti, come to demand money or to lend it on exorbitant security.

Supposing you went out for a ride and called on a friend living two or three miles away; then you returned in good spirits, but to find this tragic being waiting before your porch, and demanding in hollow accents to be paid.

Or, maybe, you were sitting in the verandah, smoking your evening pipe of peace after the usual hard day's work, and thinking all sorts of thoughts of home and bliss; thinking maybe of the *smell* of hay, and a distant cawing sound seemed to come from the rookery hard by; you did not realise that it was but the moaning of yon foaming torrent, crying ever seawards in its frantic course. Suddenly the prospect was darkened by a silent shadow, and the Chetti passed before your eyes, gliding along like a stage villain, hissing his Tamil threats, so that they just caught your ear and roused you from those sweet daydreams.

But the most gratifying sight I have yet witnessed in the whole course of my chequered career was Nana Ramen drenched to the skin, when he had not been able to bring out his umbrella because some brother

Chetti had robbed him of it. Then his tragic garments stuck to him like a glove; all that dignity was gone, and he presented the appearance of a very much bedraggled drowned rat.

Then I *was* glad.

CHAPTER VI

WAY DOWN UPON THE KEHELGAMA RIVER

THERE is hardly a tree left standing in the district of Dickoya, except along the topmost ridges of the hills enclosing the valley; here the jungle has not been cut down, because the position is too exposed for the tea bush to flourish.

Fresh trees have been planted round some of the bungalows, but they are not native trees; they were struck chiefly because of the rapidity of their growth, and partly because the Englishman could not bear to have the common jungle tree growing in his garden. Therefore he planted the Australian blue gum, and other productions which do not arrive at perfection in these damp tropics, but only present a bony, leafless substitute for the native trees.

The Dickoya valley is consequently dreadfully bare, and if it were not for the naturally pretty lay of the land, and for some beautiful high bamboos down to the river's bank, it would be tediously monotonous.

Many of the more recent planters left clumps of jungle standing, where they intended to build their bungalows, and told the Singhalese woodman to 'spare the tree' for an acre or two. Others left belts of jungle all down their plantations to keep the wind off the young bushes. But this did not prove a success, as without the support of the rest of the forest the belts, which had always been used to relying on their neighbours, got blown down by the great gusts of wind at the bursting of the south-west monsoon.

There is no doubt that trees harbour innumerable insects and flies in Ceylon. Indeed, the voracious leech lurks beneath the jungle shade, and delights to disport himself in the moisture that is collected there.

I used to be the proud possessor, with another fellow called 'The Dove,' of about six hundred acres of land extending on either side of the river Kehelgama, further down than any other estate in Dickoya, on the outskirts of the district, a long way from a village of any sort. This land was divided into two estates, one on either side of the river; it enjoyed perhaps a heavier rainfall than any other tract of land in that part.

The coolie who went daily for our letters had a tramp of nine miles by a jungle-track over the mountain to Watte Wella for the post, and in wet weather when the streams were swollen there was considerable danger attending the voyage. One day in the year 1877 the coolie started in the morning and never returned again; he was probably carried away and drowned in some mountain torrent. This was a great trouble to us, as we could not easily get another man to fill his place. There were reports afloat that the jungle was infested with elephants, and, as I said before, Tamil coolies have a deadly horror of elephants. Eventually we got one brave young man to go for one and a half man's pay, and the thing was settled.

The returns on this estate showed a rainfall of 180 inches a year. This rainfall was highly detrimental to the cultivation of coffee, as, the lay of the land being exceedingly steep, the top-soil was soon washed away when the protecting jungle was cut down. This does not make nearly so much difference with tea, which is a subsoil feeder, but with coffee it was fatal, as the subsoil was not rich enough to produce good crops of berries.

Our bungalow looked very pretty from a little distance, with a hill on the opposite side of the valley, whose summit was crowned with uncut jungle. There was very little room inside the house for anything but a bed and wardrobe in each of its two rooms, consequently washing of all sorts had to be carried on in the verandah, and we took our meals in the porch.

The Dove, my partner, had been the architect. I should recommend other planters to construct their mansions on any other plan but this, if they think of introducing comfort or convenience into their dwellings.

The river that divided the two estates was very rapid and rather pretty in parts. Just opposite the bungalow was an island, covered with jungle and abounding with leeches. This island was very pleasant to look at from a little distance.

The only fish in the river were a sort of barbel, which ranged in weight from a quarter of a pound to five pounds. They were a sporting fish to catch, but would only take a worm and not a fly. As food the Ceylon barbel is tough, woolly, full of bones, and rather stringy. I was present when one was caught weighing four and three-quarter pounds. It was a very game fish, and looked delicious when cooked—but I still regret having eaten any of it.

When we first began to cut down and cultivate the jungle lands of these properties there was no bridge over the river. In approaching our bungalow you had to swim, or if it were *very* fine weather it was possible by taking off your clothes to wade across, as the jungle-track from Dickoya came in on the farther side of the stream. I used always to undress on the opposite side, leave my clothes there and swim across, then walk up to the bungalow, call for towels, and wear one of the Dove's suits while I remained there. Then, when my visit was concluded, I took off those little garments, swam the river, and joined my clothing again on the farther side.

N.B.—I am very thin and six feet high; the Dove was rather stout and only five feet seven.

After awhile, however, the Dove instituted a bridge, and by chance constructed a remarkably pretty one, which was quite in keeping with Nature's attempts to make the place pleasing to the eye.

From the side of the jungle-shaded stream, upon which green lichens and moss congregated in damp obscurity, there stretched out from rock to rock a rustic wooden bridge over a deep, secluded pool. Here when you leant with folded arms upon the wooden paling, and looked away to where the bubbling waters ever jabbered over a little fall above, then loitered on beneath the bridge as though unwilling to leave this locality of rest and peace for the turmoil of the thickly peopled low country, you could scarcely dream that you were in the busy haunts of man, and that close beside you were jungle trees, which ere long must fall to the axe of approaching civilisation. How delightful it was, during the short span of existence which that bridge enjoyed, to lean on the rail and watch the floating dragon-flies as they hovered over the water's brink, or to contemplate the tropical butterflies wafted on the morning breeze. You could really enjoy such sights in mid-stream for awhile, out of the way of the too friendly leech.

At the bursting of the sou'-west monsoon this bridge was hurled down, broken into a thousand pieces, and carried away by the torrent.

I went down to the estate one day, and, arriving late, found the Dove entertaining the district parson.

This clergyman was supported by the planters in the districts of Dickoya and Maskeliya. He received about 350*l*. a year to minister to their souls, and to preach twice every Sunday to a collection of them in a 'coffee store.' He had no poor to look after and nothing to do with the niggers. They had a separate divine, who made a specialty of conversion and the destruction of idols; and having no other employment on weekdays but to compose his two sermons for Sunday, he went the rounds of the district, rallying the backsliders and trying to induce sinners to return to the coffee store.

Our parson was considered rather sanctimonious, and not exactly suited to a planting community. He had never been to the Dove's before, as our estate lay at the utmost extremity of the district.

We played whist after supper, and before turning in the parson proposed prayers. The Dove jumped at this, as if he had been accustomed to reading them himself every night. Then he ordered the two servants to come in, knowing that he never engaged a servant if he was a Christian; as Christianity with these dark-skinned men means education, education generally means dishonesty and thieving. Then he motioned the servants to sit down, which they did not like doing in the presence of their master, and our parson read some passages from the Bible, after which he shut up the book and knelt to pray. The servants did not understand this at all, and I heard the Dove shouting to them in a whisper behind the parson's back. 'Kneel down, d—n you, like we do; can't you see, you idiots?' The Dove himself had clothed his countenance with a saintly smile, and—being the most abandoned young villain unhung—he entered into the prayers with the utmost fervour.

The Dove was not first-rate as a planter, though he lived on the estate. He was always anxious to get away, being as good a fellow to meet at dinner as I knew; besides, he was the 'darling of the ladies,' so it was rather difficult to keep him at his work. He became very friendly with the parson and deceived him horribly, but the parson gave rather good dinners.

One day I went down to visit the Dove, and found him absent, as he too often was. I slept that night and the following night at the picturesque but ill-constructed bungalow, and still he did not return. The Dove was very fond of wandering up the valley for change of air and—'spirits.'

On the second day he came home in the afternoon. When he arrived he was in rather a funny condition, as he had been kicked on the head by a horse, and two of his teeth were knocked out; so what with a swollen head, a bunged-up eye, and the liberal potations of brandy he had been obliged to take to keep him from fainting on the way down, he seemed quite confused.

I undressed him and put him on a sofa, where he slept heavily till eleven o'clock at night; then he woke up much refreshed, ate a liberal supper, and would keep talking till the small hours of the morning, when I got him finally to bed. By next day he had quite recovered, and came to breakfast at seven o'clock fresh and cheerful, and, barring the absence of his two front teeth, he looked the same as usual.

On another occasion, when I was in Colombo with the Dove, a friend asked me to come and dine, saying that 'he and his wife would be delighted to make the acquaintance of my partner, of whom they had heard a good deal, if I would bring him too.' The Dove consented to come, and after spending the afternoon at the club with some friends, he appeared dressed at dinner time all right, except that before the meal he seemed rather cloudy in his conversation.

During soup and fish he was strangely silent, and when the entrées were being handed, we heard a smothered snore from the Dove, and discovered that he was fast asleep with his head on his shirt-front. We tried to wake him, but failed utterly, so left him sitting there dreaming the happy hours away.

When the ladies left the room we took him from his seat at table, and calling a cab, carried him out to it. The door of the cab for some reason refused to open, so we let down the window, and, shoving him in through this aperture, sent him back, with a note pinned to his waistcoat telling his servant to put him to bed.

I was a good deal put out by my partner appearing to such disadvantage before my friends, and at one o'clock in the morning went to his room at the club to curse him if he were asleep, or lecture him if he were awake. I found that he had woke up about midnight, dressed, had some supper, and was there playing billiards with some friends, much too cheery and well disposed towards men to allow of my saying anything severe to him.

That is the sort of man my partner was!

CHAPTER VII

THE PLANTER'S LIFE

SUNDAY in the coffee districts used to be spent differently to what it is in England. It was the great day for sport and visiting one's friends. It was not likely that a service would be held within one's reach more than once in three weeks, and as it was a rule for coffee planters to give themselves and their coolies a rest on the Sabbath, we generally had the day all to ourselves. Our great monkey drives were always held on Sunday, and those who had hounds made that a day for hunting the 'Sambur deer,' or the wild boar, thus combining recreation with healthful occupation and keeping one out of mischief.

The service held in a coffee store presented rather a lively picture, compared with the church service of an ordinary country village at home. There was, of course, no bell to call the slothful Christian to his prayers, and as the congregation was collected from a radius of eight or nine miles all round, some folks met at the right hour, while others joined in any time during the morning. Almost everyone rode, and as you approached the house of prayer you were likely to come on a group of 'horsekeepers' clad in white linen, tending the horses of the worshippers, and keeping the flies off their charges with a perpetual swishing of a long hair tail that they carry on purpose.

The coffee stores were very often constructed with an iron roof, and during a heavy storm service had to be suspended for a few minutes until the rain

EDWARD AND DOUGLAS INSPECTING CATTLE

abated, as the parson could not shout against the noise made by heavy rain on an iron roof.

Sunday was also a great day for inspecting cattle and cattle-sheds, just as in England. The picture is intended to represent Douglas and his friend Edward 'doing' the cattle-sheds.

Edward was the best and quietest of my acquaintances in Ceylon. I loved him with a deep and undying affection, which I still hold in the bottom of my heart.

He took me quietly apart one day, and told me all his wrongs. Amongst other things he said that twenty-six hairs had come out of his head within a week. That he was sure the rest of them were loose, and that if nothing were done he would comb them all out in a very short time.

I regret to say that I did not miss such an opportunity, but replied promptly that I thought he would become as bald as a coot; the only thing which any sensible fellow would do under these circumstances was either to apply to a Mr. Medrington, who lived in my native town at home, for half a dozen bottles of hair restorer, which must be promptly applied to the scalp; or to have every hair on his head shaved down to the roots.

The end of it was that, not having time to send half round the world for this hair restorer, I persuaded him to have all his hair cut off.

About eight o'clock one night we lit two lamps and hung them to the beams of the verandah. Edward sat beneath, and Douglas and I soon cut every hair off his head with nail scissors.

In those days Edward had the reddest of cheeks, so the white skin on the top of his head, without any hair to shield it, looked perfectly dazzling.

Two days later he had to go out into the clearing and watch about three dozen women picking coffee. The poorest joke amuses a Tamil woman, and it was necessary for a young planter to look very dignified before them. When the wind blew his hat off, it was more than the Tamil ladies could stand, as he certainly did appear very funny with his bald white head; so they indulged in a perfect hurricane of titters, and Edward was eventually forced to retire discomfited from the field.

Sundays, when the coolies were away, he did not think it necessary to wear a hat, and besides, he fancied the air might assist the growth of his hair. Therefore Edward may be distinguished from Douglas by the circle of his bald head appearing above the horizon of his shoulders.[1]

You could not with comfort stand close up to the wall of the cattle-shed, as it was very dirty, and swarms of flies found their way up your legs, so inspecting cattle on Sunday could scarcely be termed 'an easy lounge.'

A planter's life was not all 'beer and skittles.' I will now give you some idea as to how he passed his days in the 'new districts,' as this part of Ceylon was called. He rose every morning of his life at 5.30 A.M., dressed in haste, and went out to 'muster'; that is, to some central part of the estate where he found all the coolies assembled, and here he proceeded to appoint each one his work for the day, jotting down in a book how many men were to go to each kind of work. 'Muster' was only disagreeable on a very wet morning, when the coolies would not turn out of the 'lines' of their own accord, and the planter had to arm himself with a stick, and, entering their odoriferous dwellings on an empty stomach, force them to take the field by brute persuasion.

[1] Let me mention that Edward's hair did not continue to come out, which may have been owing to our treatment.

After 'muster,' he returned to the bungalow, and, having sent off the post coolie, and coolies for anything else he might require from the native village, he was ready for tea.

Tea was generally eaten at 6 A.M. It consisted of bread, jam, and coffee. In those days we always ate jam in Ceylon instead of butter, as butter was not to be procured at any price, while jam came out from England in tin pots. The bread was very bad, being made by a native man in Colombo, and then sent up to the coffee districts. We ate it about ten days old, as it took that time to be brought up in a bullock waggon, and in this damp climate it was always full of mildew, and generally full of ants also; toasted was the best way of eating it, as this killed the ants and made them more digestible.

After tea, the planter started out with his thickest boots on, and a long stick to help him up the hills. Then he walked up and down the mountain steeps, bullying the coolies, and being bullied by them, in the scorching sun, till nearly 11 A.M., when he returned to the bungalow to have a bath and proceed to breakfast.

Now it was nearly mid-day, and getting very warm; and as he sat at breakfast the insects and house flies, which were in scores, drove him nearly wild by crawling over his face and hands and tickling his neck, till he swore awful oaths, and used such damning language as he would blush to think of in cooler, sunset moments.

This is very different now, as the planters generally live in beautifully clean bungalows, where flies are not, and the kitchens, which used to be the lurking-places of insect life, are now patterns of tidiness and cleanliness. Many of them have English fireplaces, and all that brings comfort to the British soul.

I think there are few servants in an English gentleman's household at home who are humble enough to be content with a meal such as used to form the ordinary planter's breakfast. Beef was the only meat procurable, and it was so coarse, tough, and bad, that only compulsion would induce one to live on it; in this country of thunderstorms it could not be hung long enough to become tender before it came to table.

After the meat one always had a course of rice and curry, which was generally very good. The drink of the planter was bottled beer, generally Ind, Coope & Co.'s, which was brewed so strong, to keep in a tropical climate, that there was danger in drinking it.

As soon as breakfast was over, the planter started out again to look after the coolies. He found that next to no work had been done in his absence, as the Tamil coolie requires continual supervision, and the Kanganis seem to possess very little influence over their gangs, and are not able to keep the work going very much in the superintendent's absence.

To climb up the mountain side to some distant part of the estate was no easy matter at this time of day, as the sky had now clouded over for the coming storm, and the air was close and heavy from the approaching depression. A thunderstorm broke over our end of Dickoya nearly every afternoon during the five winter months of the year, between 1.30 and 5 P.M., and continued for two hours and a half. The month of January was generally rainless, but during the six summer months it rained, more or less, all day, but it was more likely to come down in the afternoon than the morning.

At 4 P.M. work was knocked off for the day, and the planter returned to his bungalow, drenched to the skin, but more comfortable, as the air had become cooler. Then he had to write down in his books how many Tamils had been at work, what each one had been doing, and what his pay was to be for the day. This took about an hour and a half on an ordinary estate, where, say, 120 coolies were employed daily. After this, it was necessary to give out medicines and dose niggers who were ailing. Castor-oil is their favourite drug, and they seemed to think it did them more good if it were poured down their throats by the master himself.

Then he had to settle disputes, if there were any, and make contracts and arrangements with head men for weeding, building cattle-sheds, 'lines,' or other works. By the time all this was finished it was getting dark, and his work was pretty well over for the day.

At 7 P.M. he had dinner, the same kind of meal as breakfast; and at 9.30 P.M., worn out with his day's toil, he retired to bed for eight hours' sleep, if he were not disturbed by the numberless fleas, mosquitoes and rats that in those days infested a planter's bungalow. Mosquitoes could be kept off satisfactorily with netting, but against fleas no bed is proof.

On five nights of the month the planter had to devote two and a half hours after dinner to estate accounts, and all letters had to be then written, as the rest of the day was fully occupied.

This is a hard life when one considers the sameness and monotony of the daily round of duties in a country without summer and winter; where every day is the same length and temperature; where the thermometer does not alter twenty degrees all the year round, and where there is no change of seasons, so pleasing to the eye at home.

But planting has its advantages compared with life in other colonies, as when the planter did get away from his work to other bungalows he was likely to meet first-rate fellows. The Ceylon planters are mostly English gentlemen, and not a collection of knaves from all nations, that one sometimes stumbles upon in the British colonies. They were wonderfully hospitable amongst one another, and a stranger travelling through these districts would probably have greater kindness shown him than amongst any other community in the world.

There were no inns or houses for the accommodation of strangers in the hills of Ceylon, except one or two Government rest-houses. These were placed at very long intervals along the high roads, say eighteen miles apart. Yet there was no fear of a traveller not getting a bed and meals on his journey: any planter was only too pleased to make the wayfarer at home in his bungalow, and set before him the best that his house could produce, although he might have known nothing of him previously. I have known a planter turn out of his own bed to make a stranger comfortable, while he slept on the floor or on a curtainless mosquito-betroubled sofa himself.

Towards the middle of May the south-west monsoon generally burst. In 1876 the tempest was more violent than usual; the rainfall in thirty-six hours registered eighteen inches at our end of the valley. It was very distressing to see the damage done to the properties after the first burst and four or five days of rain and wind were over. New roads that we had been making, culverts over which we had spent weeks of honest labour, were swept clean away; coffee trees were washed out of the ground by the score; the Dove's wooden bridge over the river had disappeared, and everything seemed to be wrecked and wasted.

It is astonishing how very bad things look the first time you visit them after the storm, when you have to wade through your estate among débris and mud in the pouring rain, compared with what they do a fortnight later, when the waters have subsided, and the sun has come out between the clouds and brightened the scene of desolation with its genial rays.

CHAPTER VIII

DOWN THE DICKOYA VALLEY

On the 26th January, 1890, thirteen years later, I rode down the Kehelgama river from Claverton to our former estate; no longer along the splendid bullock-cart road of Dickoya, but by a walking road engineered by the planters, which seemed to be constructed for walking purposes only. It might almost be said that this road was made for a party to scramble along. It was not good compared with the delightful Government roads which are now being cut everywhere.

When I at length reached my journey's end, I found the planter and his wife living in a particularly pretty bungalow. This bungalow was perched on a very steep hillside, so that in looking out of the window of the verandah drawing-room, you caught a glimpse of the garden walk immediately beneath. Then your eye travelled on down over so steep a field of tea that it made you almost giddy to look at it.

Beyond was the rushing river, here and there white with foam, as it dashed over its rocky bottom; and presently in its deeper and more tranquil parts of a deep green. In the river were such gloriously wooded islands, filled with great slabs of rock and covered all over with jungle creepers. These trees were left from the primeval forest which surrounded this gorge of the valley thirteen years previously. They occupied islands of disputed ownership, and were therefore left standing as marks of the almost undreamt-of magnificence before the valley was made the object of English enterprise.

Close to me in the bungalow were ferns all silvery and golden, shaded from the sunlight which flooded all things outside by a latticed part of the verandah. From the lines far away came now and again sounds which seemed to vibrate in the sunny air; they were the distant shouting of the nigger children's voices, modulated by the intervening distance, and the incessant turmoil of the rushing river.

I stayed here one night, and was astonished at the absence from the bungalow of our interesting little friend the mosquito. For the first time since I came to Ceylon his netting was absent from my bed.

The weather had been so glorious since my arrival that it seemed impossible that I could remember a rainfall of one hundred and eighty inches in a year; yet not only was that the case, but about the same amount is registered now, and appears likely to be the fall through endless ages. The cutting down of all these tropical jungles by the Englishman has made no difference, as the rain descends as much as ever. It is true that formerly it came in gradual showers, whilst now it comes in a tropical downpour.

There was a friend of Douglas's to whom the horse that I rode had belonged in former times. He used to stroll over some mornings and have a chat. He told us some curious circumstances relative to this quadruped. They were communicated in such a matter-of-fact way that at first I could not refrain from believing them; on thinking the matter over, however, I could scarcely credit all that was told me.

He said that this sort of horse was called an 'Indian,' and that when it was younger it had been a terrible one to 'plant.' This word sounded strange, and puzzled me a good deal. I had to ask its meaning. He replied that the horse took it into its head to remain just before the verandah when it was brought round for its master to mount.

It seemed that he came out one day, and seeing the horse waiting with the horsekeeper before the door, he climbed up into the saddle. Nothing, however, would induce the beast to advance or retire more than an inch, or, in fact, to move away from where it was standing.

They tried all sorts of expedients, but nothing would prevail on him to move. At length my friend thought of a plan, a brilliant plan, which was promptly put into execution. A fire was lighted beneath the animal, and when the flames began to make it too hot for this Indian steed, he moved about five paces, and then stood still again. A second time they kindled a fire beneath him, and when it was all ablaze he struggled off and 'planted' again, this time so conscientiously that my friend had to give up riding until the horse had grown more tractable.

He told us that this horse was very long. Before he bought it he had a most gorgeous stable built, with granite pillars and a shingle roof. But being down in Colombo attending horse sales for three months, he had not been able to look after its construction himself.

One day he wrote to the conductor saying he was

coming up country, with a horse which was to fill the new building. It did fill it till it was over full. Horrible to relate, the new stable was too short for the horse, and the tips of his ears were not concealed from the scorching rays of the eastern sun. The further end of his hocks and tail also protruded from the shelter of the shingle roof.

Then my friend was very angry and called the conductor some names, most of which I have forgotten, but amongst others I remember that he was 'an over-withered Pekoe-Sue-drinking son of a tea-merchant.'

My friend was therefore obliged to have a new stable built, at an enormous outlay, 'which,' as he said, 'just shows how easily man is deceived, and how the wisest of us poor mortals, by leaving these important items to the management of a black man, is apt to be led astray.'

One day we went for a trip in the train from Hatton to Nanu-oya, which is the top end of the railway. I say the ' top end,' because it rises the whole way up a steep incline. The station of Nanu-oya is 5,300 feet above sea-level, nearly 1,200 feet above Hatton. We left Hatton at 10.50 A.M., and after zig-zagging along through an apparently endless multitude of tea estates, we arrived about one at Nanu-oya, in the district of Dimbula.

It was quite distressing to encounter nothing but tea all the way. The hills would be exceedingly pretty if they were only covered with jungle, or if they had anything else growing on them but this interminable tea. Unfortunately there *is* nothing else, except on the highest crests of the surrounding mountains, and there nature seems to assert her rights with patches of beautiful jungle, which vary the scenery, and cause a soothing influence to the eyes of sinful man.

It is extraordinary to look over the Dickoya valley, a valley which only thirty short years ago was completely covered by a vast solitary jungle, amid whose labyrinth of moss-grown trees there was no road, and scarcely a trail. Here the huge 'Doon' raised its straggling limbs aloft, and a mass of tropical creepers intercepted the way to all else besides monkeys and an occasional elephant. There was a silence that might be felt over all things; and, beyond a mosquito or two, the half-starved leeches seemed the only indication of life.

To see this valley now, with scarcely a tree left standing, but with its many well-engineered cart-roads, its estate roads, and thousands of drains; to see the white pillared tea factories, the bungalows, and the tea estates ranging over the hills, is a wonderful sight, but it is no longer picturesque. During that day's journey how we longed for one acre of 'patna' to vary the monotony of this ever-green tea.

The station of Nanu-oya was brand new, and so terribly English that it did our hearts good to go to the native shops and find the native Singhalese selling native fruits out of a native kaddy.

It is curious to notice how this railway line circulates amongst the thousands of acres of tea and coffee plantations in its upward progress, and winds in and out like a snake amongst the bushes. At one place we came right over and in sight of the line which we had left miles behind; yes, far, far down below we saw the tail of the serpent swinging round beneath.

The carriages were divided into square compartments, about double the size of a broad-gauge compartment on the 'G.W.R.' in England.[1] They had three armed cane-bottomed seats on either side, with windows behind, and one seat between the two rows with its back to the engine, holding in all seven people. If you are sleepy or ill at ease from any cause, I do not know anything more hopelessly wearying than these pillowless seats, as they have absolutely no support for the back of the head. If you fall asleep your head rolls out of the window behind. If you try to lie down on three seats in a row—which is possible—you find that you are occupying too much space, and someone else is sure to come in, with no end of tin boxes. This makes such a clattering, and fills the air with such an execration of coolies, that sleep is out of the question, and you have to get up and make room for the new-comer. Besides, these trains are generally too full to allow you to lie in comfort on the three seats, so that it is necessary to sit bolt upright, to face into the glare of the opposite windows, and not to mind the friendly chattering and chaff that is going on among the six other planters who are your fellows in adversity.

However, for a picnic, as we were going, I do not know that you could come across any picture more delightful than our carriage presented. We had taken a table with us, and absolutely quantities of food. There was our hamper filled with all that the Claverton cook's most cunning machinations could contrive, and another hamper with a pie in it. Even now that I

---

[1] The gauge of the Ceylon Railway is 5 ft. 6 in. The G.W.R. broad-gauge is about 7 ft., while the English narrow-gauge is only 4 ft. 4½ in.

am back in England I often think of that pie. When I am bored to death sitting in a hard-seated, hard-backed pew, pretending to listen to a long-winded sermon, then I think of that pie, and it gives me comfort somehow in the chilly stone-floored church.

We had with us plantains and the egg-shaped tree tomato, mangoes and pineapple. Taking it altogether, with the coolness of the hill breeze and the slow

THE MORTARED, WHITEWASHED LUMP OF CLAY
(See next page)

motion of the train ascending those tea-covered mountains, we spent a very jolly time.

Going up the line we came to a station where lots of coolies turned out from our train, and we noticed one young Tamil girl, got up in her best red-and-yellow-checked summer costume, descend with two live chickens, one under each arm. These she had brought with her on an outing, because she was afraid they would be stolen if she left them behind to wander about the home 'lines.'

Talking of chickens reminds me of a fact which seems to throw a veil of inanity over Tamil coolies' Hindoo worship. There was a Swamy-house close by Claverton; merely a thatched roof on poles, beneath which were two little whitewashed pyramids, on the tops of which were placed earthenware saucers. What these saucers might have contained I do not know, as when I visited this sacred spot they had nothing in them.

I was told by the owner of the estate that the coolies who constructed these sacred pyramids had built up inside each of them a *live chicken*, and let it perish for want of air, so that you may say with the poet:

> 'Stranger, pause, and shed a tear:
> A gruesome deed was acted here.
> Beneath this mortared, whitewashed clay
> A fowl was foully put away.
> Hidden beneath this sordid block
> Lies our old friend, the barn-door cock.'

CHAPTER IX

THE 'BOPATS'

I was watching some coolies playing cards on a Sunday morning, from a point of vantage whence I could not be discerned. It was very comic to see the four naked figures squatting on their calves—as only the nigger can squat—on the sunlit ground, with a piece of sackcloth instead of a card table. They seemed full of chaff amongst themselves, while the old conductor sat in a verandah round the corner with his spectacles on, writing in an enormous book. He looked up now and again to utter many Tamil expressions, in a loud authoritative voice, to some coolie women and children who were busying themselves near by.

Away in the distance the banana leaves were being blown about, as though a hurricane was at work on them; really it was only the mid-day breeze which was stirring up their long feathery leaves.

Then the hens—for there are always fowls where Tamil coolies are collected—were wandering about engaged in busily scraping up the sunbaked clay; or jerking themselves forward as they talked to one another, each thinking herself the only chicken in this great world.

There was a little girl sitting on a stone before the old conductor's house, feeding herself from a bowl of rice, and the great big chickens *would* keep coming up as if they thought it was their bowl and not hers; so that she could scarcely keep them off with her hands, as they seemed so remarkably tame and were so persistent in their adoration of the rice.

THE OLD MALAY CONDUCTOR.

A little way off two children were wandering about among the tea bushes, perfectly naked, not feeling the sun in the least, but laughing a sort of merry childish laugh which was pleasant to hear. Here a girl came by bringing on her head a brass 'chatty' filled with clear water from the stream, and there lay the inevitable thin coolie dog, a poor beast who never gets anything worth eating, and does not know what the smell of a bone is like, he gets one so seldom. How these poor dogs live, stretched out at full length in the sun all day in this condition of ruminant vacuousness, is a mystery. It is truly said that we live by eating, and many a dog that I know lives simply for eating; but these poor dogs, if they have come into the world with any such intention, have long ere this found out they must live to sleep instead; they seem to sleep in order that they may live as economically and as quietly as possible.

Looking at it from my point of view on this day, Ceylon seemed to be a peaceful sunshiny country, where it was delightful to idle away a few long weeks of life. But I really knew that your happiness in this land all depended upon whether the 'dhobi' had brought your clothes from the wash lately or not, as that was an occasion which generally turned the summer of life into a dismal winter-time of bitterness. As you looked over the shirts, which so few short weeks ago had been brought freshly out from home all spotlessly white, starched and new, you found them now ruined by his exertions over the purling streamlet. When you saw the lack of starch, the frayed cuffs, and noticed how your shirt-fronts were torn away by brutal struggles with the stones at the frothing brook side, you found that in spite of sunshine and these valleys laughing with crops, life was not all bliss even here.

Watch a dhobi at work; see him dashing your best white shirts against a rather rounded stone by the stream. He has nothing on except his loin-cloth, because he perspires so freely. Watch his exertions, as with both hands uplifted he swoops down with your shirt upon the stone; and then you tell me that there is no black man in Ceylon who works half as hard as an Englishman.

When Englishmen say that coolies are poor creatures without any gumption in their build at all, it goes straight home to my heart, and I see what a maligned being the Singhalese man really is.

The highest part of the estate where I was sojourning in Dickoya was just 1,200 feet above the river Mahavelaganga, which rushed by rapidly at its foot. From this eminence one got a glorious view of Maskeliya's jungle-covered mountain tops. Here and there a bit of smooth slab rock was seen, which had proved too hard, slippery, and steep for anything but moss to grow on its sides. Beyond were the forest trees, with their magnificent branches rising up in an apparently never-ending maze; while nearer to me were ruddy tinted leaves showing brightly against the dark-green foliage of the jungle beyond, making in all a beautiful picture.

It was here that we saw the tracks of an elephant quite fresh upon the tea-bush-covered soil. This elephant only lived about ten days from that time, as he was shot by a planter when roaming foolishly about the ridge of the adjoining estate.

The ordinary elephant of Ceylon has no ivory tusks worth mentioning, and is therefore useless when killed. It is necessary to shoot them whenever they come out on the estates, as the coolies are in such desperate terror of elephants that you cannot induce the men to go forth and weed or pluck tea when the tracks are at all recent.

On February 12 I gathered that long brown horse from the stable, and after bidding adieu to my grieving friends, I was borne swiftly away from Claverton's sheltering grasp, and travelled far up the Dickoya valley till at length I came to Eltofts in Bogawantalawa.

What a name the further end of Dickoya possesses; but what a much more beautiful name is that of the stream which tumbles down over its rocky bottom! It is called the 'Bogawantalawaoya,' a name which has become so familiar to me now, that it seems like nothing to say it right off, and I give way to its many-syllabled and somewhat tangled mass without even a quiver in my voice; for is not use second nature?

Here they showed me many things with which I was—strangely enough—already familiar. There was a factory in which the machines were turned by a turbine, and we tasted, with a grave face, about fourteen of the bitterest, strongest teas that you can possibly imagine.

One morning we went to the 'Bopats.' After climbing uphill for two mortal hours, we got within a stone's throw of the Bopats. We had been mounting up, first through a large tea estate, with blue gums planted along the roadside. These trees are intended to give shade, which in any other country they may do; in Ceylon there is far too much rainfall in the year to suit the blue gum, and planting them seemed to have been a waste of time. However, you see their smooth mildewed stems everywhere.

Then we penetrated a quantity of dense jungle,

and at length got out on to another tea estate, up which we struggled, till at last when we had passed a tea factory, a pretty bungalow, and a number of Tamils picking leaves, we came to more jungle.

I had intended telling you about the Bopats, but must say, with the parson, 'My friends, let us pause and consider,' for surely it was too hot, and the sun was scorching our backs too much to rush on. We had now got up many feet above the Bogawantalawaoya, and looking down the zig-zag steps from the gorge we had ascended, we could see over the tree tops the far-away coffee and tea fields, to where great patches of jungle and patna were lying sweltering in mid-day heat. Above us were trees with branched heads of leaves in great clusters, as they towered aloft against a background of granite walls. These walls were so steep that man in his most aspiring moments could never think of scaling their weather-beaten sides.

We clambered up the pathway and felt like ants creeping up a moss-covered wall, till at length the summit was reached, and we found ourselves suddenly on the Bopats. They were apparently endless grassy downs with sloping hillsides, and every now and then jungle rising out of them, while in the distance rocky mountain peaks rose above this beautiful undulating ground.

We wandered over a grassy plateau, it appeared to me for miles, and at length beneath some huge rhododendron trees, having descended by imperceptible degrees, we came to a stream, where three Singhalese men were washing for gems. They had dug a pit beside the water's edge, and from this grave they ladled basketfuls of mud and sand. Then, sitting on a plank with their feet in the water, they rinsed all the mud out of the baskets, and left in the bottom a few handfuls of quartz, which they looked carefully over in hope of finding untold wealth. I suppose it would be needless to remark that while we stood and watched them nothing of any value was found—nothing, in fact, except pebbles and sand.

We remained about half an hour watching these gemmers; then one of us said, 'How delightful this

SINGHALESE MEN WASHING FOR GEMS

existence must be, sitting on a wet board all day with your legs in the cool water, sifting, ever sifting, your bosom swayed with the hope of eventual success, and your manly form exposed to the rays of the sun, only five degrees from the equator! Then when the rain comes on you retire to your jungle home, where you chew " Betel nut " till it is over.'

It is needless to remark that there is nothing these naked Singhalese men fear like rain, absolutely *nothing*. They go and live away amid the jungle leeches, and rather seem to enjoy baffling their attacks; but give them a couple of spots of rain, and off they go, never mind how precious the stones may be they are finding.

The gemmers had built a couple of what might be termed altars on the banks of the stream close by the scene of their labour. They were a description of small dolls' houses, standing on poles about five feet from the ground, and well roofed in with talipot leaves. Beneath the talipots were what we will call some seedy offerings, as they appeared to consist of the seeds of a reed, and were doubtless placed there as a propitiatory offering to their gods. Why they should have been put to the trouble of erecting altars, or whether the gods were satisfied with their talipot roofing, we shall never know, as we were Christians, and these natives were presumably Buddhists, which makes a difference.

Then we turned homeward, and found it much easier work walking down the mountain slopes than it had been crawling up.

On one occasion we scrambled through some leafy scrub and got down to a natural cave close by the river's edge. The roof of this rocky cavern was plastered over with swifts' nests. These swifts in Borneo are called 'callocalid,' and their nests 'neottopteris.'

The garden swift of our English homes does not exist in the tropics. I believe the Bornean swift is smaller than a British swallow. It makes a nest of weeds, feathers, and saliva; a glutinous saliva which fastens the nest to the overhanging rocks. These nests must be worth nearly forty shillings a pound, for the Chinese make soup of them. Bird's-nest soup is an article I am totally unacquainted with, but I understand the Chinese are very fond of it. They only cook the glutinous saliva, and not the feathers and weed.

We gathered two of these nests, for this was not the season when the birds were laying. The nests were packed carefully away in a tin box amongst my clothes, where I thought they would travel securely,

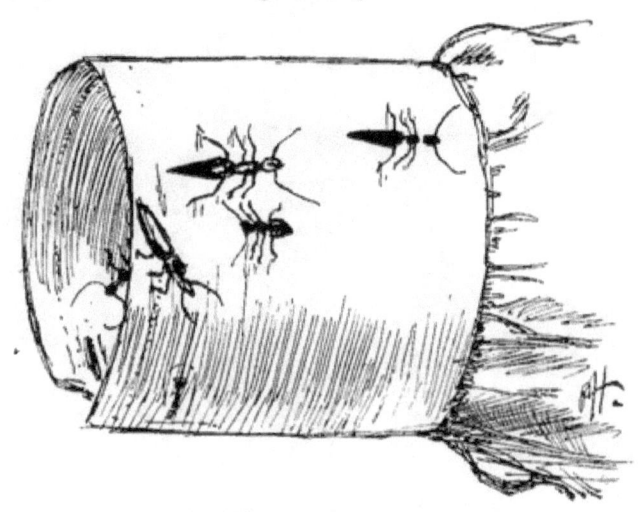

THE ANTS ON MY SHIRT-SLEEVE

and as they were clean and stiff I did not even trouble to wrap them in paper. On opening my box at the end of its journey, a feeling of horror crept over me when I saw an ant—yes, a small black ant—creeping out quite unconcernedly from beneath a vest. Then I took the contents of the box to pieces, and found some more in my pyjamas; but what they particularly seemed to fancy was my sponge, as this was full of them.

I thought these insects would drown easily enough, and did not bother about them, but left my sponge unmolested for the night. However, in the morning they seemed to have increased amazingly, as I saw them running here and there all over my white washing stand. I discovered them in what appeared

THE STICK INSECT

to be hundreds issuing from the recesses of my cupboard, and when I dipped my sponge in the water it did not kill them; they actually liked it.

I was then torn with doubts whether a life infested with ants was worth having, or if it would be better to put an end to such a miserable existence.

In spite of this I live on.

Talking of insects reminds me of one which I discovered adhering to my person when I was down by the river which runs through Claverton. I suddenly observed something moving clumsily about near my ear. It was impossible for the animal to get nearer, as the length of its body (seven inches) prevented its crawling between my shoulder and my 'solar topee.' It had probably crept on to my hat from some overhanging bough. I snatched this creeping thing away and examined it closely. It was emerald green all over, and exactly like a bit of bamboo. Its six legs were very minute in circumference, and came out almost at right angles to its body. This object is called a stick insect, and is the most distasteful-looking creeping bug, and the largest, I have ever seen.

CHAPTER X

IN THE LOWER COUNTRY

On February 15, leaving Eltofts, I came down the valley again to Claverton. This was the day of the Dickoya race meeting, and no Englishman in the whole of the district could get a moment's work out of the coolies. They went down by thousands, dressed in perfectly clean white cloths, to attend the races! Every man, every woman, and every child who could walk, was to be seen tottering down towards the course. Mothers, with babies which should have been in arms, slung their children, wrapped in white 'sarongs,' on to a pole; thus with one end of the pole over their husband's shoulder and the other over their own, they marched along.

Many of them went ten miles or more from the estate to the Darawella racecourse, and then back again the same day. Coolies were packed round the little district course in *thousands*, not betting on the races as we Englishmen should do, but looking on it, we supposed, as some religious ceremony. It was strange to look round the little Darawella flat and see Tamil coolies in a white and black mass packed up to the top of the hills which surround the course.

It happened to be a beautiful summer day, and they appeared to enjoy themselves in a quiet way to the utmost—more, in fact, than the planters did; as although there were plenty of ladies present, still these British ladies were separated from the men, and remained seated in a little throng by themselves during the whole performance.

On March 2 I left Douglas's bungalow and the valleys laughing with tea crops, and went down to the Peradeniya Gardens, to Kandy, and to Kondesalle. Peradeniya Gardens are quite beautiful, but I shall not mention these, as they have often been described before.

From Kandy I was driven about four miles to Kondesalle Ferry. It was a pleasant drive through a perpetual Singhalese village, which is at first a town, but which soon becomes scattered, with dwellings about every hundred yards.

Singhalese people cannot exist as the Tamils do, in 'lines' perched up on treeless tea estates; they have to live beneath shady boughs, so that the whole way along this road there were cocoa-nut and other trees, reaching right away from the road as far back as the eye could see. This was not a great distance on account of the mass of leaves which surrounded you.

After driving some distance alongside the broad river 'Mahavelaganga,' we came to the ferry, with a collection of Singhalese houses on its steep bank. The ferry-boat was a combination of two ordinary dug-out canoes gouged out of tree stems, connected by boards nailed across them, and paddled by an almost naked Singhalese man in the stern.

At the ferry the river is about two hundred yards broad. Here it is a sluggish stream lazily dragging its waters along with scarcely depth enough at this season of the year to cover its sandy bottom. We soon stemmed the river, and having reached the further side found a bullock bandy waiting to take us two miles to the abode of one of the planters.

This journey was accomplished mostly under the shadow of tropical trees. We were now only about 1,300 feet above sea level, and a good many miles from the coast, so it was terribly hot. On this level there were no tea plantations, as the climate, together with the soil, renders it possible to abandon tea and to introduce instead cocoa bushes, Siberian coffee, ordinary coffee, indiarubber trees, cotton, vanilla, and tobacco. All of these I saw growing in what seemed a subdued confusion.

Now and again when we came across a plot of ground belonging to and planted by natives, it was filled with Jack fruit trees, cocoa-nuts, plantains, and tomatoes, growing helter-skelter, and looking as though not planted but indigenous.

There was no natural jungle here; all the trees seemed to have been planted by natives, and were lacking that natural beauty and those deep, quiet jungle shadows which exist higher up the country. One missed the thick shade from lofty trees which falls across the feathery cardamoms on the forest edge. The cricket's loud call, singing his hymn of praise to the dazzling sunlight, was absent. There was no bubbling streamlet to sound its plashing in your ears.

I have noticed in streams that come from the jungle there are dark transparent pools with beetling insects ever whirling round in irregular circles; pools in the depths of which one sees a layer of quartzy sand, or a

darkness occasioned by decaying vegetation. Little ferns peep out from cracks in the dark lichen-patched rocks, and the intensely green or yellow-tinted leaves of the cardamoms are reflected with the blue sky above in the sombre waters. A little lower down dried and crackling foliage falls into the purling stream. These streams are spotlessly clear, for they flow from the uncut jungle on the mountain tops, and find their way down amid the drooping foliage.

Here and there pools have been formed, and if you look into those crystal depths, besides your own reflection you will see quantities of minute animalculæ and fresh-water crabs wandering about beneath miniature slabs of rock.

But I must return to the bullock bandy in which we started away trotting to the bungalow.

It is wonderful how these bullock drivers propel their bullocks. They seem to goad them along with sounds only. When accompanied by ladies and gentlemen they cannot of course practise the cruelties common to Singhalese bullock drivers. The Singhalese make a noise exactly like the grunt of a pig, at the same time twisting the bullock's tail in a way that must be exceedingly disagreeable to the poor beast.

Our driver was a Tamil who had been taught by his English employers, so that he only dared hold up his stick in a threatening attitude; I never saw him strike with it. Our bullock kept up a subdued trot from mile to mile on end, and when he was asked to stand he just stood without so much as flopping his ears, and scarcely swishing his tail. He stood often quite quietly for an hour, either in the sun or the shade, it made no difference which. In fact, this was the most interesting and domestic bullock I have ever known.

The accompanying portrait of his head should give some idea of how he looked when he stood calmly waiting for what would happen next.

When I got up to the bungalow I found bullocks, bullocks everywhere, and not a drop to drink! This is not strictly true, as there were plenty of deep wells,

THE TROTTING BULLOCK

but the rainfall was very light compared with that in the tea districts. There were, however, no horses hereabouts, but everything was done with bullocks. There were four bullocks to turn the machinery in the store, and bullocks to carry water from the well to the bungalow—in fact, where estate roads were so satisfactorily cut they could have bullocks everywhere.

There is one charm about Kandy in addition to the scenery, which is, the fire-flies at night. After dark every bush and tree is alive with floating phosphorescent light. They are around you in countless myriads of light, floating about in ever-moving gyrations.

A gentleman came out from home a few weeks before I was in Kandy who was making a study of human skulls, and as the Weddas of Ceylon are said to be the oldest race now extant on the face of the earth, he wanted very particularly a Wedda's skull. He therefore travelled far into the country till he came to the abode of this almost uncivilised race, and through an interpreter said what he had come for. The man interpreted his wishes as follows: 'This Englishman wants a Wedda's head, for which he will give you eight pounds of tobacco and three pounds of the best beads.' The Weddas then looked wise, but did not say anything or do anything. So the Englishman got the interpreter to repeat his desire, but not being able to get any response went away in disgust.

About three weeks after this he arrived at the hotel in Kandy, and found a very high parcel wrapped in banana leaves awaiting him. On opening it, it proved to have a partly putrified Wedda's head in it. Whether they had killed their fellow man, or if he had died a natural death, will always remain a mystery. I believe this is a fact.

CHAPTER XI

MOUNT LAVINIA

WHAT a sweetly pretty address this place has! It is 'Mount Lavinia,' Dehiwala, and the only other postmark my letters had on them was 'Oalkissa.' I should think from reading this address that it must be a second-rate heaven in disguise.

It *is* a pretty promontory, lying about nine miles from Colombo along the sea-coast, and jutting out into the ocean away from the unbroken forest of cocoa-nut palms. If you could come to it on one of those cold east-winderly days in England, you would think it quite a paradise on earth.

The ground round the hotel is covered with a kind of short grass, which makes it look green and bright right down to the sea. On the top of this green knoll a former governor of Ceylon built a villa; it is a handsome building, and stands about fifty feet above the sea. After he left Ceylon it remained untenanted for some years, and then a railway was made down the coast which passed close to it; an enterprising Englishman bought the building and turned it into an hotel.

It is a large well-built house and makes a capital hotel, so close to the sea that you have only to step out of the door, walk twenty yards down the green

BULLOCKS AT KONDESALLE

slope, and you come to the rocky coast against which the boundless Indian Ocean continually dashes.

The railway runs from Colombo to Mount Lavinia, and the station of Mount Lavinia is only about two hundred yards from the hotel. You can run thence into the metropolis in about half an hour.

To the right and left of the promontory stretches a sandy beach with cocoa-nut palms growing right down to its edge, and their roots running into the sea. These sands look most attractive from a distance, but are not really agreeable to walk on, for they are soft and allow one's feet to sink in at every step, making a journey over them most fatiguing. Quantities of insects most hostile to man are ever disporting themselves on this briny shore.

The climate at Mount Lavinia is so muggily hot, I would say if it were English so damply hot, that although I fancy the thermometer never goes beyond 86° even on an April day, still the moisture evaporating from this shimmering sea is very damp. Indeed, so damp is it that unless you take your clothes out of the tin box which contains them every three days or so, and hang them up in the sun to dry, it is impossible to keep the mildew away.

The shore between Mount Lavinia and Colombo is perfectly flat and a trifle uninteresting, with nothing to look at but palm trees, the sand, and the sea, therefore a walk along the strand is rather a monotonous proceeding, without any rocks or picturesque excrescences of any kind. They did say that there used to be a shell somewhere along the coast, but one afternoon a native man picked it up and gave it away. Now there is nothing to disturb the peaceful serenity of that vast expanse, which stretches away to Colombo. That desert area is abandoned entirely to the roots of the cocoa-nut trees, the playful flea, and the crabs.

Ceylon is a wonderful country for crabs. There are land crabs in the hills, and sand crabs on the shore.

When I was taking my walks abroad one morning,

THE SEA COAST

what should I see but about three million black-crabs-picked-out-with-red-points, sitting together on a small rock, and seemingly immersed in the contemplation of their own gorgeous persons.

They looked at each other and smiled disdainfully as they saw me approaching, but did not say anything —I do not think that crabs ever talk much one with another. Evidently they thought that I should be afraid, as there were so many of them congregated

MARCH 1876

together. They just stood on the top of that rock in a cluster, showing off their red points and looking

MARCH 1877

haughty, till I jumped on to the place where they were thinking, and then they ran for their dear lives.

In referring to a journal which I kept when I was

in Ceylon in 1877, I notice the following statement:
'May 10.—Left home for Ceylon, *via* America, this day year; both myself and my luggage are considerably demoralised since then. My case of rods has gone home; one of my portmanteaux was given to a chambermaid in Salt Lake City, and my other cases have dwindled away to nothing. My hat-box was thrown out of a porthole, being of no further use, as the top hat which it contained is being worn by the boots at the Brevoort House in New York. I always found it too small, but he had a little head. My guns have become rusty, my clothes misshapen and faded with wet and sun. If you were to take the contents of my tin box away, I should be left to roam the earth clad like a nigger.

'Thus it is in life.'

There are numbers of crows at Colombo, and many more at Mount Lavinia. They are wonderfully tame—so tame, in fact, that you dare not leave your room or go to sleep in it with your window open, as they would be sure to come hopping in and take away any jewellery and pins that you happen to have left on your dressing-table.

When you are sitting in your easy-chair and have dropped off into a doze, you may be suddenly awakened with a start by the hoarse cawing of a thin black object with an enormous shiny bill slightly on one side. He hops on to your looking-glass off the window sill, just to examine, and see that you have not left anything of value about. He has a dark brown neck and throat, and his prominent beak is terribly long, black, and defiant in appearance. This is the crow.

One day a man let off a fowling-piece near my

window, and on looking out I saw that he had killed one of these hoarse-croaking birds. Immediately an innumerable multitude of cawing black objects came from everywhere, so that the air was in no time *thick* with winged blackness. All the taller branches of the trees had tens and twenties of these birds on their flat tops. Such a cawing went on, as each flying bird talked the matter over with the other flying birds, that you could not get in a word edgeways. Although this foul deed had been perpetrated in their very midst, they could do nothing as a retribution to the man; and eventually they went away leaving the air a good deal clearer by their absence, but still agitated by their distant cawing.

In Ceylon, especially in the low country, these crows are the public scavengers. You see them everywhere. They get very daring where there are settlements, as they soon learn that the natives will not harm them; and the Englishman is scarce in many parts of the island.

I have seen an old crow fly down and take a piece of bread out of a child's hand, as she was walking with her nurse on the road. If you leave a biscuit or anything edible on the table in your room, and forget to shut the window, you may be quite sure you will not find that biscuit on your return.

Supposing I opened my window at Mount Lavinia and threw out a morsel of food, at once about ten or twelve crows came flying round. They came from distant lurking-places amongst the *débris* of the new buildings, and from the housetops. I think that they can see a bit of biscuit right through a brick wall, and smell a morsel of carrion when they are about

145 miles away from it. I might continue throwing pieces of biscuit out, and was quite *sure* that none

CROWS AT MOUNT LAVINIA

of them would ever touch the ground, as these crows kept flying round and round, and *catching them in the air* before they had fallen two yards. A feeling comes over me that no one will believe this, but it is perfectly true.

All day the hoarse caw of phlegmatic old crows was wafted to one on the summer breeze from their resting-places amongst the cocoanut branches.

I have heard a great deal about the brightly-plumaged birds of the tropics, and I have read that birds with most brilliant feathers are to be found in India and Ceylon. Probably there must be birds of this description somewhere, but I have never seen them myself. If Emerson Tennant and other authors say there are such birds, of course there are.[1]

One day, on emerging from a cocoanut plantation, I came on a bit of broken wall, on the top of which a bird was standing, and showing a wonderfully clear outline against the blue and boundless ocean beyond. The scene was so striking that I could not help exclaiming with the poet,

What bird *is* this with feathers gay?

Of course I could not really deceive myself. I was perfectly aware, in spite of the poesy which filled my soul, and found vent in mutterings such as these, that it was only a specimen of the domestic crow.

We tried shooting the crows with a rook rifle, but they took in the situation in a moment and avoided us. We never got a shot, though we lay in ambush all one afternoon under the shadow of palm-trees, waiting for them to alight.

It occurred to me whilst waiting thus that a crow

[1] Oddly enough, you cannot find them on the sandy cocoanut-planted land which extends for miles in every direction inland from Mount Lavinia.

must be a bird of remarkable decision, for this reason. When a crow approaches a cocoanut-tree he does not falter or pause for a moment, but goes straight for one leaf and settles on it. Supposing there are one hundred cocoanut palms on half an acre of land, and each tree has thirty-seven leaves on it, does it not seem wonderful that a crow should be able in a moment to select one leaf out of so many, and make straight for it? I call him a remarkably clever bird, but then Ceylon is a wonderful country and Ceylon crows *are* exceptional.

There is no tide at all in Ceylon. The height of the sea along the coast is, like everything else in the island, always the same; except that when the monsoon changes it makes a slight change also. The extraordinary thing is that the sea on this coast rises two or three feet during the north-east monsoon, and falls again during the south-west—although the coast faces right into the south-west, and the wind is about twice as strong during this monsoon. The rivers also that flow out on this coast carry about three times the volume of water during the south-west monsoon that they do during the north-east. But as the ocean is pretty vast here I suppose they could not raise it much even if they did their best.

As I said before, Mount Lavinia is a pretty place, being a little promontory surrounded on three sides by the sea. Its connection with the cocoanutty land is very small. When you have wandered on to the main shore, you see an irregular mass of cocoanut trees, an interwoven chain of light bark stems, all of the same thickness, as these trees do not, like our English trees, get any larger with age, but come out of the ground apparently the same circumference as they mean to continue until their dying day. A young cocoanut tree is, indeed, a beautiful thing,

ABOUT THIRTY-SIX FEET FROM THE GROUND

having all the thickness of a full-grown tree; but it has *more* leaves, and these leaves are just as large, as feathery, and a lighter green.

One day I was watching a coolie climb a cocoanut

tree and pick a lot of cocoanuts from the top. The coolies climb these trees in such a clever way that I should like to try it myself very much. They tie their feet together with a loose piece of rope, and then go up like a caterpillar, doubling themselves up and undoing themselves all the way. But if I tried to imitate this mode of climbing, I suppose I should have to begin by dressing myself as the natives do for the occasion.

The costume is exceedingly simple, consisting of a hat only and not another stitch of clothes except a bit of 'loin-cloth,' which means a morsel of rag round their waists. Besides, they have the rope which ties their ankles together, if you consider this clothing. I give a portrait of a gentleman shinning up a tree (as the Yankees would say) in pursuit of cocoanuts.

I have also tried to give some idea of the owner of the cocoanut trees. Sometimes he used to stand with his hands folded behind his back almost all day long. I could see him in this position whenever I looked out of my window. This dotard would stand thus silently on the shore, always expecting a boat to come in from the sea, which never came.

Sometimes he went fishing in the early morning with a casting net. He stood with his simple fishing costume on, watching the sad sea waves as they came tumbling in, in great long rollers.

There was a knowing look in his eye, and he had

the net thrown over one shoulder ready for action at the right moment. His attitude reminded one of some noble beast of the forest—a tigress, ready to leap on its prey—as he waited there patiently expectant, looking for the wave that was to bring him the fish he intended to capture.

On a sudden he darted forward and threw the net out in a circle over a dancing wave. Then he cautiously drew it ashore so as not to let a single fish escape. Now he examined the net to see what luck he had had. Behold there was nothing. There never was anything. I watched him very often at this occupation, but I honestly confess I never saw him catch a fish.

A look of disappointment then settled on the old man's face as it naturally would, but he did not give in. Fresh every other morning he came to his work, I am sorry to say always with the same success.

Beneath the young cocoanuts, immediately below the hotel on the landward side, a Sambur deer was tied and feeding; at least she was not feeding all the time, as at intervals she licked a young fawn, or came putting her long tongue into your hand. This was a tame deer. Indeed, it was the fault of everything on this green bank of loveliness that it was too tame.

When I was out on the lawn before the house, one of the donkeys of the place, which was wandering about quite close to the building, suddenly came up over the quiet lawn and took a bite out of my sleeve. Then this restless ass (bent on doing mischief) went up and disturbed one of the landlord's deerhounds which was sleeping in the shadow of the house. The poor dog did not like this at all, and said so; but the donkey stood there, the incarnation of all that was aggravating, with his ears back, bobbing his head forwards and backwards. By his looks I gathered that he intended to say to the dog, 'If you do not move out this instant, I'll kick you,' so with a howl of disgust the dog decamped.

Talking of dogs reminds me that training into Colombo there was a sight visible from the carriage window which, although occurring frequently, still fills one's soul with a very sad feeling. Three terrier doggies were being washed by their two dog-keepers in the sea. Why I infer that this filled my soul with disgust is, that the dear dogs disliked being operated on in this way so *very much*. Some dogs love going down to the seaside and madly plunging in of their own accord after sticks, but still they cannot bear being submerged beneath its waters by a common nigger man.

Truly I yearned over those poor little dogs, who, although it was not cold, were shivering. I could not help observing the piteous expression on their faces as they were being wiped over with towels. It made me almost weep to see them with their tails between their legs, and their eyes almost closed, yet running down with tears, meekly giving way to the overbearing scrubs which were administered by these wretched black men. Leave me weeping.

CHAPTER XII

SOMETHING ABOUT THE NATIVES AT MOUNT LAVINIA

THE sea at Mount Lavinia looked brimful of katamarangs (native boats). It seemed to be overflowing with them. These boats came gliding on through

KATAMARANGS ASHORE

the restless waters of that bright Indian Ocean, till they arrived at the shore, where they did not appear to stop. You would think that any ordinary minded boat would stop when it got to the land, but these katamarangs kept heedlessly sailing on up the sandy beach till at length they rested beneath the cocoanut trees.

I could not at first think how this was managed, but presently one of the boats came in, and I saw that the sails were kept up while six or seven men pushed it on to the sandy shore till it was out of the reach of the sea. Even then—in this wonderful country—they do not trouble to pull the sails down. There would be no use in doing this, when the wind comes from exactly the same direction and with almost the same force six months in the year. The fishermen leave them up, with a steady breeze bagging them out, till they want to go sailing out again.

The next village to Mount Lavinia is called Angulana. It is the largest fishing village in the island of Ceylon. I went there one day and watched an aged native sitting beneath a cocoanut shed selling fish.

Quantities of fish were lying about, and men kept plunging their skinny arms down into the bottom of boats—where their feet never go, as the hollow trunks are infinitely too narrow and deep to admit of this—and bringing forth all sorts of fish. The most noticeable of these were 'Tunnyfish,' about three feet long. This old gentleman was not only crowded with buyers, but he had on quite his go-to-meeting expression as he scornfully took the pennies from the natives who showered them in. I should have said that this haughty old gentleman was the ordinary salesman for a certain number of boats.

There were several Singhalese on the sandy ground playing cards beneath the shadow of cocoanut trees. They were playing quite a different game to any that

I had witnessed before. It had this redeeming quality, that the men smiled over their game as if they enjoyed it; and although they were playing for coppers, they did not drink, and apparently did not quarrel as our fishing population would think it necessary to do at home. Eight dark and almost naked natives sat there upon the crabby sand, with their legs bundled away under them—in a position that no European can think of, much more perpetrate —playing a game of cards of which I could make neither head nor tail. I suppose that its intricacies were not hidden from them, for they smiled so cordially as they handed over the coppers to one another. I could not but think that it was the easiest game in the world for the nigger man to understand.

These natives were sitting near a cocoanut shed— everything was cocoanutty down there—the roof was made with the brown weather-beaten leaves, the walls were constructed of leaves plaited together, and the posts made of cocoanut stems. They sat on a cocoanut leaf mat, they drank out of the shells of the nut, and if you said you were thirsty, they caterpillared up the trees and plucked green cocoanuts for you to drink. The cool bright milk of the green nuts was very refreshing.

I will give an extract from my journal of 1877.

'I thought that I would like to go out fishing on the high seas with a native man in a native boat, but the sea looked so horribly rough that I was nervous. One day a native boat came in from a fishing expedition and disgorged its freight on the shore just below the hotel, when the fish were, as usual, sold by auction. I was present at the sale. Then joy entered my soul that I had never started on a fishing cruise : for, until that day I had not been aware of the nature or dimensions of the denizens that I should have had to contend with. I was horror-struck to see them pull out of the boat no less than fifteen fish of the most ferocious and strangest aspect that it is possible to imagine. They resembled fish which I have seen men carrying about on poles in Chinese pictures. In the same way Singhalese salesmen carry fish, one at either end of a pole, probably because they are afraid to get nearer to them.

'If you can picture to yourself such a horrible scene, imagine what my feelings would have been had I—in ignorance of the nature of these fish—gone out to capture them. Supposing one of these denizens of the sea, refusing to be abstracted from the water, had seized me unarmed and almost alone in our little craft, and carried me away down, down, helplessly clasped in his slimy jaw, to lowest hell, there to make sport of me with his demon satellites.' I have attempted a sketch of the situation, in which I presume that the native fisherman 'stands in with the green-eyed monster.'

All niggers seem to have a wonderful tendency to 'perch' themselves. In the low country they sit on a rail and support their extended arms on their knees, their legs being folded under them in the position of a frog about to spring. I think this is done to avoid the ants and flies that infest the ground.

Up country there are not apt to be convenient rails, so that they generally settle down on a log or stump when they want to rest. I made a study of a

Singhalese and a Tamil man fishing, poised in what they considered a comfortable position, and in a be-

'ELP!! 'ELP!!

coming attitude, but my publishers, oddly enough, did not think it sufficiently attractive for insertion.

They will sit like this for hours, pursuing some mild occupation, or pensive, enjoying the thoughtful sunshine.

They seem to have much more power of utilising their feet than we have. I suppose—as they never wear boots—their feet become much more supple than ours. They can cling wonderfully to a rail when 'perched.' They can climb up a cocoanut tree or walk over a wet log in a most surprising way. They will use their toes for picking up a knife or stone from the ground, where we have no power to move ours.

A new wing was being built to the hotel at Mount Lavinia, and by looking out of my window I could see the works going on. The Singhalese contractor was a very good-looking man. His name was Alus Appoo.

The Singhalese men draw their long hair back off their faces, and tie it up in a sort of suppressed chignon behind. They wear a yellow tortoiseshell comb in their hair, which looks from the front like a pair of rather saturnine horns.

The only way a new-comer has of distinguishing between a young Singhalee man and a young girl is, that a man wears a comb, and a woman does not. After a stranger has been in Ceylon a short while, he discovers another difference—viz., that a Singhalee lad is very pretty and feminine-looking, while the young girls are short and exceedingly ugly.

The Tamils in this respect resemble Europeans, as their women are decidedly good-looking, while the appearance of the men is comparatively ugly and honest.

There were also a number of Tamil women at work on the new building. They were mostly employed in carrying basketloads of sand, for making mortar, from the shore to the works. Many of them had one or two babies with them: little naked trots of from one to three years old. Some carried their infants on their backs, others left them to sprawl about among the brickbats and mortar, while they went down to the shore for the sand, and returned to chide their babes after each load. *All* the women talked and scolded the whole day through, and the mammas had intervals of ten minutes constantly, to suckle and tend their offspring.

The porters on the railway between Colombo and Mount Lavinia wore a most becoming costume— viz., a suit of blue serge, jacket and breeches, with a red cloth sash tied round their waists, and a kind of smoking-cap, also of serge, to protect their heads. They thought themselves great swells got up in this way, and most of the porters in and near Colombo affected the English language. They all carried white cotton umbrellas, to keep their clothes dry in the rain and keep up their dignity with when the sun was shining.

There was a sort of head porter at every station, who wore a white belt in addition to his other garments, and altogether clothed himself in haughty superiority. His belt hung over one shoulder and round his body. I noticed one day, when I went to Colombo, that the head man at the Fort station carried in his hand a linen handkerchief with a border of lace round it. Imagine a nigger and a railway porter with a lace handkerchief. These coloured men *never* use handkerchiefs, as the art of blowing the nose as we do it is at present unknown to them. This porter was a Tamil man, but he cultivated a moustache, which Tamil men seldom do, for the very good reason that they cannot. They rarely have any hair on their face at all. The Malays almost always have a moustache and nothing else, while the Singhalese all wear a thick beard.

One morning a Singhalese man came and per-

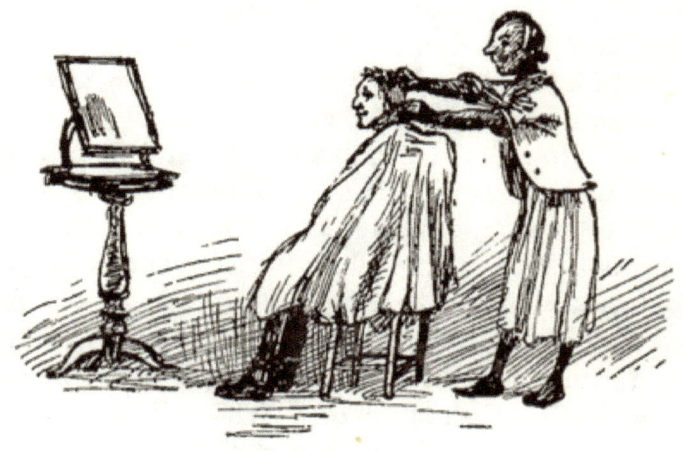

HAIR-CUTTING

formed on my head. This gentleman had devoted his life to the science of barbery. He was then getting old, but had certainly not attained perfection in his art. I dare say he found this foreign and barbaric occupation uphill work, as the Singhalese never cut their hair, except perhaps once a year, when they tie it up with a piece of string, as you would a horse's tail, and chop it off level. However, he pushed on manfully, slicing people's chins and making terraces of their back hair daily for his daily bread. He stood a long way from his victim, as though he were afraid of your pinching his legs when he came round in front. I fancy he was not so much at home lopping off one's locks as he would have been mowing down a stubbly beard with the patriarchal razor that he carried in his belt. I never allowed him to try this latter operation on me: having submitted to one experiment seemed more than sufficient.

One day, when I was down here in 1877, a Mr. Johnson made himself known to me and was very civil and chatty, as he said he had met me somewhere before.

Mr. Johnson slept in the next bedroom to mine, and as the rooms were all open at the top for the sake of ventilation, as in Colombo, I could hear anything which went on in Johnson's room.

One morning he said to his servant who was helping him dress, ' Boy, I begin to think you *must* be rather a fool; you will play the very devil with my finer feelings if you don't take care. This is the second time you have cut your *beastly* hand stropping *my* razor.'

Then ten minutes later I heard this: ' It concerns me to think what a fool you are getting. When you chew betel-nut, I must beg that you will not spit on my clean shirt-fronts.' After a pause he continued, ' Of course the red mark produced by your careless ejection of saliva is of no consequence on other parts of the shirt, but I fear that you will render the garment useless for the time being, if you will persist in spitting your betel on to the front.' From this last remark I presumed that there was a red mark on his shirt-front.

Both the natives of Ceylon and the Tamils are

very fond of chewing what is termed 'betel.' The following information was obtained from an English-speaking Singhalese in Colombo, and I am not sure that it is correct.

They take the green leaf of the pepper-vine, which is called by the Tamils betel. It looks something like an English vine-leaf, and is about the same size. In this they fold up rather more than a saltspoonful of ordinary lime made from coral, which is called by the Tamils 'chunam;' to this they add some scrapings of areca-nut and flavour it with the seed of cardamoms. With this combination in their mouth they chew and spit all the time between meals. Englishmen who have tried it tell me there is no virtue in it, but perhaps the nigger would find no virtue in chewing tobacco.

Mr. Johnson was in business in Colombo, and was away there all day, coming back to the hotel in the evening to dine and sleep. He came into my room early one morning, and said he hoped I would make any use of his servant I wanted while he was away during the day. I thanked him, and he added, 'The fellow isn't much good, but (here the boy came into the room, and Johnson, fixing his glittering eye on him, said sternly) if it amuses you to watch the behaviour of a being quite bereft of sense, it may be gratifying to observe this fellow at his work.'

It was very kind of Johnson to lend me his servant, but considering I never had enough occupation for myself, I did not know how I should keep this boy employed. At first I felt like a host with a troublesome guest on his hands and no amusement with which to divert him.

Presently this young man came and told me a long story about his relations having come down to Colombo for one day, and might he go and see them? Then I was delighted, although I feared it was a lie. I said, 'Go, my friend; minister to your aged relations all day long, and may God speed you.' So he went.

I did not suppose that, because his expression was somewhat sinister, his soul was ill at ease. He always looked as if he had swallowed a crayfish, claws and all, having in his absent-mindedness omitted to remove the shell. Besides, he had espoused our religion and taken a Christian name, 'Samuel.' We know from missionary books that those who act thus are always happy; generally they die young and go straight to heaven.

There was a young gentleman I knew up country, whom let us call Tom.

One day, when I was reading the paper in the sitting-room at Mount Lavinia, who should come in but Master Tom, with three Burgher ladies, all dressed as we used to say at school 'up to the nines;' Tom, with a frock-coat and tall hat, and the ladies equally beautiful, but more showy. He seemed rather embarrassed at seeing me, as of course he had no right to be down there escorting ladies about, but ought to have been one hundred and fifty miles away on his estate driving coolies. I believed that Tom was engaged to be married to one of these Burgher girls, or else he was not engaged and ought to have been; it was always rather a shadowy affair, and I could never quite get to the bottom of it. He was very unwilling to acknowledge any engagement, as they were an attorney's daughters, and partly black.

Tom had brought his *fiancée* with her mother and sister to lunch, hoping he would come across no one he knew, and seemed far from pleased at finding me.

Seeing that he was uncomfortable and did not introduce me to the females, I said I was sorry but I had to go away on business. Then I walked down to a small Singhalese town about four miles away and came back by train.

On arriving once more at Mount Lavina station, I alighted on the platform, where four persons at once caught my eye running over the bridge from the hotel to the train. Three females and one male were occupied in this way. When they came nearer I saw that they were Tom with his top-hat in his hand, and his frock-coat tails flying in the wind, followed by the three Burgher ladies whom he had brought to lunch. They passed me in a state of profuse heat and visible perspiration.

I hallooed out to them in passing, 'Lots of time, the up train is not in yet.' They thanked me, and slackening off their pace walked into the station, just in time to see the train go off without them.

I am not naturally vicious, and did not mean to do those backsliders any real harm, but I was in error.

I saw them no more except through a window, when they did not look pleasant, and I silently prayed that Tom might be killed in a railway accident when the next train went to Colombo, or that some casualty might prevent us meeting in this world. As it happened we never did come across each other again. I hope that this introduction of the incident will not remind him of the circumstance.

MOUNT LAVINIA

There was very little to amuse a visitor at Mount Lavinia. He had either to eat, sleep, or do nothing. These pastimes palled on one after a while. It was comparatively easy to kill the morning when one was fresh and capable of understanding anything, but towards midday, when the thermometer stood at 89° in the shade, and everything seemed parched with heat, life sometimes seemed almost unbearable.

Supposing you had eaten lunch and become tired of reading, a monotony crept over your perspiring existence which rendered you rather hopeless and despondent.

In the evening things freshened up a bit. Fellows came back from Colombo with the latest home telegrams. You had news from England of your mother-in-law's death, or other incidents which brightened up your future. Then there was dinner to be eaten, and the temperature fell a few degrees, which made life more bearable; at least, more bearable until ten o'clock struck the hour for retiring to rest.

Going to bed in these balmy climes is not nearly so much trouble as at home, because you have not so many clothes to take off. When you are stretched on the mattress, there are some foreign creatures which at times make sleep very difficult. Fleas are the chief nuisance. I am a light sleeper, and therefore cannot remain torpid when attacked by more than half-a-dozen at once. It would be rather a good plan to water one's couch with tears, as they used to do in the Bible. I think that a flea would feel uncomfortable finding himself the centre of a rather large, and an unusually salt, tear.

One night, just as I had turned into my fleaey

I

shake-down, a reptile in the shape of a centipede crept up my arm, and inflicted two wounds. These inflamed and made my arm swell for a couple of days, but as I succeeded in killing the centipede I did not mind so much.

NEAR MOUNT LAVINIA

Fleas were not the only objection to a sojourn here, as in addition you could hear everything that went on in the whole house; the rooms, as I said before, being open at the top.

Some questions which puzzled me much at one time were: Has an hotel servant any right to have the hiccoughs at night? Is a visitor at an hotel in the colonies justified in complaining to the manager about it?

Supposing a servant has the right to create this alarming misery outside your bedroom door at two o'clock in the morning. What advantage does he derive from keeping himself awake, merely that he may annoy anyone who happens to be within reach of these gastronomic sounds?

How was I to reprimand the man, if I could not speak Singhalese, and he did not understand English? Could I stone him with boots and books till he went away?

When one hiccough was over the anticipation of the next, to me lying awake in my bed, was something awful. I thought that I would count to ten and see whether it came. No, not yet. I counted five more, still all was silent. I began to think the malady was over for the time, when another spasmodic cough arrived and fidgeted me out of my life.

I knew that if it went on much longer I should be a lunatic before they came to call me in the morning. Happily, a thought occurred to me, which I at once adopted. It was a jug of cold water. . . . He was gone, and the passage outside my room was an inch deep in water. Well, I thought, it should have soaked in before morning, and in the cool grey dawn be refreshing the gold-painted cornice of the saloon-ceiling below.

One night my rest was again disturbed. I was awakened at about 2.15 A.M., by hearing someone rattling at the handle of my door. As this continued for some moments and no one came in, I said, 'Who is there?' There was no answer, and the rattling still went on. As I knew that my door was not locked I hallooed out, 'Come in if you want to, but don't stand there making that noise.' Again no answer; so I got out of bed and opened the door. Outside I found a youngish man in evening clothes, with a candle in his hand. This young man I had noticed at dinner with a party of strangers. He immediately said, 'Oh, I thought this was No. 14.' I replied, 'It is No. 14. What do you want?' He said, 'Oh, I beg your pardon; I've m-made a mistake,' and went away.

I turned into bed, but presently I was disturbed again. There was more rattling at the door, so I shouted out, 'What the dickens *do* you want?' Then I got up to go for that miscreant; but the scoundrel, who had returned this time without a candle, had hold of the handle of the door outside, so that I could not turn it, and, therefore, could not get at him.

Presently, by keeping quite silent, I heard him walk off, but discovered that he had found the key on the outside, so had locked me in and gone away. Then I *was* roused. The blood of one of my uncles, who fought in the battle of Balaclava, seemed boiling up in my veins, and I shouted till nearly the whole hotel were awake, till someone came and loosed my bondage.

Then I took the door-key, and, entering the room, double-locked the door, not omitting to bolt it; also I shut and bolted my window, as I knew that I had been contending with a lunatic. I thought that he might return in the still night-watches, and make life hideous to me again. There was a parapet, broad enough to walk along, outside the window; this was why I bolted it.

How he knew that my number was fourteen I cannot tell, as, on inquiry, I found that he was a stranger here. The rooms were only numbered in the manager's brain and on the books. These numbers dodged about in the most promiscuous way.

The lunatic left early next morning, and I joined my prayers with those of his well-wishers for his speedy dissolution.

CHAPTER XIII

TRAVELLING IN CEYLON

When in Dickoya, twelve years ago, civilisation had not reached its present perfection.

The following may give some idea of the sort of troubles the planter had to contend with in those days.

One day in June I went up country and found the whole of Dickoya clothed in a tarpaulin of perpetual rain clouds, which crawled over the mountain tops and shed humid misery on all the district throughout my stay of a few days there.

On the last day of my visit I walked up to a bungalow in the afternoon, where I was to dine and sleep, and arrived there at about four o'clock. The manager of the estate, whom we will call Mack, was leaving the district of Dickoya for good on the morrow; and he had been asked out to a farewell breakfast with his wife at a neighbouring bungalow.

On my arrival I shouted in vain for a servant, but the place seeming quite deserted, I took possession of an armchair in the drawing-room, where I patiently waited a couple of hours till Mr. and Mrs. Mack came home. When they returned we found ourselves in the following interesting situation: Mr. and Mrs. Mack were both wet through, not in the English sense of the word, but drenched with tropical rain; they were sick and headachy from poisonous champagne they had been *obliged* to drink at the parting breakfast. The servants, in the absence of their master, had stolen the key of the wine cupboard and were all lying on the kitchen floor hopelessly drunk. The Macks were expecting some rather smart people to arrive in half an hour, who had been also asked to dine and sleep.

None but colonists can look these sort of domestic trials in the face calmly, but in this wonderful country—where in those days everything always went wrong—we were equal to the occasion.

By a little after eight o'clock, a party of six of us sat down to a moderately good cold dinner. We were all dry, cheerful, hungry, and full of hope. We had one servant, that two of our friends had brought with them, to wait on us. So we got through that evening remarkably well.

The following day we journeyed down to Colombo again; Douglas, Mack, and myself making the party. The drive down to Navalapitiya was—as usual at this season of the year—remarkably wet.

Douglas, who was sitting with his face away from the horses, of course talked cheerily all the way. Unfortunately his chat was once interrupted by the horses giving a sudden start forward, when he was shot out into the road, taking a square tin box with him. They both fell right into a 'horsekeeper' who was running behind the carriage, and the two got mixed up together with the box on the road, and had some difficulty in disentangling themselves. Beyond this we had no accidents.

Mack, who spoke Tamil and Singhalese well, seemed to derive some satisfaction from swearing in these foreign tongues at the bullock-cart drivers, who never would get out of the road for our carriage to pass. Every now and then he would hop out of the bandy with the whip in his hand and clear the way forcibly; using, what we guessed must be strange oaths or blood-curdling threats in Singhalese, as his face got, if possible, redder than usual with the exertion.

It was in those days a laborious task travelling in the tea and coffee districts of the island, but not nearly so bad as making a trip along some of the roads in the lower country, where bullock-carts were not generally used.

On reaching Colombo I slept the night in one of those rendezvous for mosquitoes and lizards which happily no longer exist—viz, a 'native-kept hotel.'

The following morning at five o'clock I left again by a so-called 'coach' for a place called Ratnapura, which was at that time rather out of the way. Why the vehicle in which we travelled was called a 'coach' I do not know, as it was only a native-made waggonette drawn by a pair of horses. The seats were narrow and very slippery; the back was an iron rail; and if you want to know to what a pitch human misery could be brought on earth, you should in those days have taken a ten hours' trip in the Ratnapura coach.

I was crowded in with three natives; one a Chetty as black as your boot, while the other two were Mahomedans, who presented a kind of yellowy brown colour all over.

I offered my *vis-à-vis* a cigar, so as to make

THE BAMBOOS. FROM WARLEIGH FORD, DICKOYA

friends with him. He smelt it and passed it to the next man, who also smelt it and looked it all over, then passed it to the third man who, sacrificing himself to science, bit off the end and smoked it; after which, as the Yankees say, 'he reached around and spat.' With this harmonious pastime he continued to amuse himself for nine blessed hours, till we at length arrived at Ratnapura, and the journey's end put a stop to our misery.

The cruelty with which the horses were treated on this journey is more than I can describe, and I hope I may never see such a sickening sight again as they presented at the end of each stage. If there be a hell for lost souls, I hope the nigger drivers of those coaches may be compelled to occupy the corner next the fire when they go there.

I was very glad to leave the coach at the end of our ten hours' sit, and at Ratnapura Rest-house they treated one very well.

They gave me a novelty in jams, a nutmeg jam which the old man told me he made out of nutmegs from trees in his own garden. It was a hopelessly sweet and tasteless compound.

The next morning I had breakfast at the Rest-house, and after breakfast asked the Rest-house keeper if I could buy a pipe in the native village. He said 'no,' but he could sell me one himself. I asked, 'Was it new?' He said quite delightedly, 'No, not new,' and he went and fetched it. He was right; it was not new. It was an old very-much-smoked meerschaum, with a dirty piece of silver round the stem. I did not buy it, as I did not 'kind of fancy' the look of the thing; which surprised and disappointed the old man.

From thence I walked on a great distance—how far I do not exactly know: I think it was about thirty-one miles. The journey took me two days to accomplish. At length I found myself about 2,000 feet above sea level, on a new clearing that had just been opened, called by its owner Townhope.

The last day's walk had been a very tiring one, almost entirely through rice fields and cheenah thickets. This cheenah grows on land that has been cultivated by natives, and which has been grown over by a kind of high thorn bush with prickly stems, something like the blackberry bush at home, but a good deal higher. The paths through the cheenah are not quite high enough for the European to walk through without stooping. They are cut by the natives, who are generally a much shorter race than we are. In this case there were six or seven miles of cheenah, which made travelling quite exhausting.

The rice fields are merely tiring to walk over for a long distance. It is very annoying to keep slipping off the ledge which divides one level from another, and to get your feet wet through in the hollows whenever you slip.

I found my friend Manly very cheerily living in a small hut made of planks, the inside of which was about twelve feet square, containing no furniture but a camp bed and some boxes for seats. He had written saying he could not put me up, but as I had not received the letter, there I was, and very glad I had come. Happily I had brought a hammock with me, or I should have had nowhere to sleep. After dinner we rigged up this hammock. The first time I essayed to lie flat in it the ropes broke and I came down to the floor on my head, but eventually we succeeded in fixing it up rightly.

Here I spent a fortnight, and we had a very pleasant time together. We saw no other Europeans, as Townhope was an isolated clearing in a vast forest of jungle on the mountain side, and no one else lived within some miles of the hut.

We used to go out with guns and search for game whenever there was time and the coolies did not claim Manly's attention; but we always came home covered with leeches, wet through, thoroughly worn out, and unsuccessful, but not disheartened.

We were told the district was famous for sapphires, and we spent one or two afternoons in the river's bed with baskets searching for them, but never found anything of real value. It rained every day, but not all day, which was fortunate, as Manly's hut being very small, we only turned into it for the purposes of eating and sleeping. The rest of the time was spent out of doors.

Meat was difficult to obtain at Townhope, and always as tough as leather when it came to table; but the boy made excellent curry, and we cut down 'Kitool palms' and ate their young shoots boiled for vegetables. Manly had laid in some tins of Dundee marmalade, which helped one wonderfully with the musty bread. With Manly's huge form and cheery face opposite me across the board, I manage to ' 'tice down' quite my share of the meals.

CHAPTER XIV

AT MANLY'S

AFTER I left, however, Manly had some very fair sport, as, in writing to me the following November, he gave me a graphic account of how he had with three hounds run down an elk or 'Sambur deer,' and eventually stuck it with a knife in the river. The river ran through the jungle about a mile and a half from the one-roomed bungalow.

He had also shot one or two so-called 'red deer,' and a good many jungle fowl and hares, all of which must have been delicious food in that country, remarkable for the scarcity and toughness of its beef. His letter went on to say: 'There are now about 230 acres of land felled and opened here, and, as you know, I am the only Englishman living in these parts.

'I had very hard work to clear the land, and it was all done with borrowed labour. One connection of about 500 coolies refused to work, and I was harassed into using strong language. They tried to "hammer" me, but by the greatest piece of good luck I got the better of them.

'The trouble had been brewing for one or two days, till one morning the head Kangany was very insolent, right out on the far side of the Donhead clearing—about two miles from my bungalow—away from my own coolies, and in front of his lines (huts). He called me all the names that he could think of; names which are not down in the Tamil dictionary.

'I managed to keep my temper, as I knew how it must turn out if I did not, and told him quietly enough that he must go back to his estate on the following morning. That I should stop all his pay. He replied that any way he would have something for his money; and aimed a blow at my head with a large stick, which must have finished me if I had not guarded it with my cane. Then I closed with him and succeeded in throwing him over a pretty deep ravine.

'At this moment I saw a man coming towards me with an uplifted " alavanga " (crowbar). I waited till this fellow got within a few feet, and then kicked him straight in the pit of the stomach. He threw up his arms, screamed and dropped his alavanga straight into my hands. Just then I was knocked down from behind with a "momety," for now the coolies were all round me and quite close up. However I at once managed to get on my feet again, and close in front of me was the Kangany whom I had shoved over the ravine, but who had managed to climb up again. I felt very much as if I was drunk from this fall, but I just had sense enough left to deal him a blow with the alavanga, straight across the face. He was insensible for two days.

'The coolies then ran away in every direction; but presently turned round and pelted me with stones. However, I burst through them towards the jungle, got into an overgrown ravine, and cut like a hare to the bungalow. They lost me in the jungle, and being new to the place had to go back round by the road. I met them at the bath-room with two loaded guns, and swore I would shoot the first man who passed the conductor's hut. About twenty-five of my own coolies now came, and pelted them with stones till they left the ground.

'The next day some policemen came and took away all whom I could identify. They were eventually brought before the magistrate, pleaded guilty, and got as heavy a sentence as he had the power to inflict, which was a very light one. The magistrate advised my taking the case before the Supreme Court, when the punishment would have been much greater; but it was too long and too expensive a business for one in my position, so that I could not do it.'

You see that in those days life was not all beer and skittles in Ceylon.

Altogether, I was away ten days, and then determined not to go back by the same route, or to suffer the anguish again which had been my lot with the three black men in that Ratnapura coach.

Having, therefore, walked down to the Rest-house, I took my passage on board a coffee barge which was to convey me fifty miles down the Kalloo Ganga. I agreed to pay the owner a pound if he would land me at a place called Bolgodda, which was only a drive of ten miles from Moratooa station on the Mount Lavinia line of rail. I had to take my own provisions with me, and the accommodation was, speaking mildly, very inferior.

At one o'clock I walked down to the nearest bend in the river from the Rest-house, and found the barge moored alongside the bank ready for her passenger. I went on board provided with beer, bread, eggs, and tough chicken, also a clay pipe and some second-rate tobacco. Then we started on our journey.

The boat was propelled by four naked Singhalese coolies, who rowed with heavy 'sweeps'; there were some more men to steer, and others to swear, as they aped the English bargee in this particular. There was also another passenger, a Singhalese man, who could speak a little English, and he proved very useful to me, as, of course, I did not know a syllable of Singhalese.

The barge was full of coffee, except in one small space at the end, where a place was cleared for us to sit. This was covered with a cocoanut-leaf roof, and beneath this a board for sleeping on was laid down, with two cocoanut mats over it. On this board I became torpid at night, as, what with the awful heat, and the mosquitoes, the hardness of my couch, and the six niggers lying alongside me, I got very little sleep.

We were all obliged to crowd under that scanty cocoanut-leaf roof as it rained hard during the night, and the heat in our berth was something terrific.

The river Kalloo was exactly the same the whole fifty miles that I went down it. It is very pretty to look at once, but becomes monotonous after the first few minutes. There are highish banks on either side, completely covered with plantains, bamboos, and palms, with creepers growing up the stems of the trees, and hanging down in great clusters over the water, the whole presenting a tangled jungle of the greenest green. But there is no change. Each fresh bend in the river presents another stretch of the same monotonous tropical beauty, and one's eyes soon tire of this verdant scenery.

However, I enjoyed my trip very much, as the weather cleared a little, and at night there was a moon shining brightly between the showers. The combination of sunshine and moonlight, clay pipe and bamboos, produced a very peaceful and soothing effect on me, weary with travel.

The natives paddled on till about half-past eleven at night, when they moored the barge alongside the bank. Then everyone, except the mosquitoes, reposed till early morn.

About six they were up again and working steadily on down stream, till at twelve we moored against the north bank at Bolgodda. Here I disembarked with my baggage and got a bullock hackery to drive the ten miles to Moratooa station.[1] We changed bullocks once on the way, as no Ceylon bullock ever goes more than seven miles at a stretch. We drove the ten miles in two hours.

The bullocks used for this purpose are very small, only about the size of a donkey, and have a hump on their backs. They are brought up from their mother's lap to trot, and trotting is their profession. They can go about six miles an hour, and are able to trot for exactly six miles, then they stop. So that if you wish to make a journey of fifty miles, it is necessary to find out first how many times six will go into fifty; if you can discover this, it is possible to calculate how

---

[1] I had to pay about 2s. 6d. for the hire of the hackery, which, I believe, was nearly double what a native would have paid.

many relays of bullocks you will require to perform that journey.

The bullock hackeries are so low from the floor to the top of the cover, that there is hardly room to sit upright with your legs dangling over the road.

You have to take your hat off inside these vehicles, and it seems most inconvenient, as there is no place to put a hat. The seat, which is the most slippery thing—except ice—that I have ever unwillingly slid along, has no ridge to prevent anything sliding off it

A BULLOCK HACKERY.

and on to the ground. If you put your paraphernalia into the network which is slung beneath the bandy, it gets filled up with dust, kicked up by the heels of the bullock; or you may find the net is not strong enough to bear your camera-legs, and hat, and gives way, causing untold dust and misery.

In case of rain there is only just room for one man to crouch under shelter; even then he has to double himself up in the position of a frog about to make a spring if he means to keep dry.

The Government of Ceylon have instituted turnpike gates all along the high roads in the low country, at a distance of about five to seven miles apart: therefore the natives have instituted post-houses for the change of the bullock hackeries all along the roads, one on either side of the turnpikes. By this simple arrangement they can drive from Galle to Colombo (seventy miles) without paying a single toll.

A native drives his seven miles; leaves his bullock hackery at a near post-house; walks through the bar and takes another hackery on the further side. Then he drives to the post-station on the near side of the next pike, and so on all the way, walking through the pikes and driving the distance between each.

CHAPTER XV

DEPARTURE FROM CEYLON

But I have frivoled away long enough in Ceylon: let us go on towards Borneo, whither I was bound, and where I was not led to expect much. A gentleman who had been out there told me before leaving Ceylon that Borneo was ' a dashed half-Crown sort of place: ' which in fact proved to be true, as it does only half belong to the British Crown.

I left Colombo on Sunday, March 9, in the Nordeutscher Lloyd steamer 'Preussen,' and made my way to Singapore.

It took us five days' screwing at the rate of thirteen knots an hour to reach this port, and I wondered to myself if I should not be deafened with music before arriving there. They had a brass band on board which played the *whole* day long in the loudest tone possible in our over-decorated saloon. However, eventually we steamed into Singapore unhurt.

CHAPTER XVI

A SHIPLOAD OF EMIGRANTS FOR NORTH BORNEO

AFTER a stay of some days, the time came for me to be quitting Singapore, so I said good-bye to the tame honey bear in the hotel gardens, and a great deer which was just like a dog with his friendliness to man, and left.

From Singapore I went to British North Borneo, to Labuan and to Brunei.

Nearly all the Chinese population of Singapore seemed to be aboard the 'Ranee,' going down with us to Borneo. On the decks of this little steamer there were no less than 360 Chinamen and Malays going to be Bornean coolies. I am only speaking figuratively when I say that there seemed to be nearly all the population of Singapore, as I am told that there are about 500,000 Chinese in the city alone; but in looking round our decks you would think that the whole of Singapore were trying to crowd themselves on board.

The air seemed thick with the smell of Chinamen. I believe that it is the smell of opium-smoking which makes the Chinese nationality seem so disagreeably aromatic. Any quantity of human beings cannot of themselves smell as strongly as these folks did, without the assistance of opium.

Each coolie emigrating to Borneo pockets an advance of about 5*l.* before leaving Singapore. Besides this, 10*l.* has to be paid by the landowner in North Borneo to the commissioners for coolies who are to stay three years on an estate. When they had pocketed their 5*l.* the coolies' great object used to be to get off the ship which was taking them down to Borneo before it left port, so that they might enlist again and pocket another 5*l.* In consequence of this, the ships now steam out a little way from port as soon as it gets dark, and anchor about three miles from land; as far away as possible from all boats, so that the coolies may find it impracticable to swim.

In spite of this, one of our Chinamen did jump into the water late at night, as we did not leave the roads finally till 9.30. Our captain was not told of this occurrence till about twenty minutes after it had happened, so that he could not discover the whereabouts of that sinking Chinaman. Then one of our passengers said to the mate, 'He'll have a pretty long swim before he gets ashore, won't he?' To which the mate answered, 'He'll have about ten fathoms to go before he arrives at the bottom. I reckon he won't reach anywhere else to-night.'

This was the only Chinaman that we lost on the trip except one. His tale was rather peculiar from our British point of view, but perfectly ordinary from a Chinese.

He was sitting one night on the railing which surrounds the ship, and he happened to drop off, first into a doze and then into the sea. The rest of the Chinese who were round him thought this such an ordinary occurrence, that they did not say a word about it till the following morning, when there was a 'muster' of Chinese coolies and one was found to be missing. The head man then asked where he was, and ever so many men said, 'Oh! that Wee Chunk, we saw him drop into the sea, we suppose it is he who is not here.' Thus these sublime mortals look on a death as the most ordinary occurrence in life.

If we had been told he had fallen into the sea, as it was a calm night we should have lowered a boat and picked him up, thereby saving the estate to which he was going about 15*l*.

Perhaps we should have also afforded the Chinamen some pleasure; but there is no knowing in this deceitful world if we are all built alike or no. These Chinamen are so hopelessly Chinese and unlike anything which has been brought up under European influence, that we cannot understand them.

On our way out of port we passed numbers of steamers lying in the roads of Singapore. They were painted white, green, and black, and flying the flags of various nationalities. Amongst others was a flag that I had never seen before; it puzzled me, as I could not make out to what kingdom the steamer belonged. It was a yellow flag with a broad cross on it; one side of this cross being black and the other red. She looked a very neat little steamer of about 700 tons register, and, on approaching nearer we saw that she was called the 'Rajah Brooke,' and this was the flag of Sarawak.

The second day after leaving Singapore we came in sight of some islands called the Sirhassen Islands, and eventually we steamed quite close to a mountainous headland called Koti, which is the most northerly point of South Natuna Island.

These islands belong to the Dutch, but at present, I believe, have not been taken any further notice of except the fact being generally known that Holland holds them under her thumb. There is no government, and there are no Europeans living on them—nothing, in fact, but a savage naked Malay race. Ships are not in the habit of coming here from Singapore, as this track leads nowhere except to the island of Labuan.

The Natunas are biggish islands [1] and are inclined to be hilly, though the Southern group are not mountainous.

It seemed to me a pity that such an apparently fertile spot should be under Dutch rule, or perhaps it would be better to say 'marked in the maps as Dutch.' They have now been some years

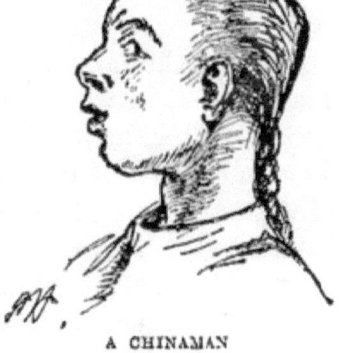

A CHINAMAN

under the beetling eye of Holland, but at present the natives do not know what a European looks like.

But to return to our Chinese coolies. Some of those aboard ship were good-natured-looking enough, but from what I have seen of the Chinese coolie, I should say that he very seldom smiled, and never laughed. It does not seem to be their nature to laugh.

Of course they had not any more hair on their

[1] The largest being about the same area as the island of Majorca, in the Mediterranean.

faces than a buffalo has on his back; indeed, they had less: aboard the ship, where they had not been shaved for a week, you could see this easily enough. I shall have something to say about a Chinaman being shaved when we return to Singapore.

They all had a long pigtail, which was wound for convenience round their head, but I think they only wore their hair bound up in this way when at sea. Then for dress, each Chinaman had a black linen pyjama jacket and trousers. The trousers were so baggy that each leg was more like a woman's petticoat, coming down within a couple of inches only of his ankles.

Every Chinaman had a long, narrow wooden box stained red, in which all his possessions were stowed away. When he wished to unlock it he inserted a huge key and turned it first forward two-and-a-half rounds, this struck an alarum which gave seven tings; then he turned it backwards half a round, which gave two tings. At least, this was the plan adopted by a Chinaman who resided close to my chair on deck. I constantly heard other boxes being opened with the same click of the alarum which announced the proceeding.

Picking one's way along the decks amid the thick multitude of Chinese life which was exposed there, one saw them playing cards very frequently. I do not know if they were playing with two packs or with only one, but their packs consisted of infinitely more than fifty-two cards. They were little slips of cardboard about three inches long by one inch broad, covered over with Chinese emblems in black. Four men played cards together, all sitting cross-legged on grass-made mats spread one over the other; they played for copper coins just as the fishing population did in Ceylon.

A little further on some Chinamen were engaged in 'skinning' the rind off sago roots (which resemble turnips) with their long *nails*; then eating the roots greedily and with evident enjoyment.

They generally messed in knots of four together, when they consumed any quantity of rice, dried little fish—which from our European point of view looked exceedingly tough and bony—and hard-boiled eggs, all of which were ladled down with chopsticks. These chopsticks were merely two little bits of rounded wood about as thick as a pencil. The end which they put into their food was stained pink, and the other end, which was green, was interlaced in the fingers; both ends being flat like an uncut pencil. How they can get the contents out of the *shell* of a *hard*-boiled egg with two little rounded sticks and put it gradually into their mouths, it would be difficult for anyone who has not had the advantage of seeing it done to imagine. I only know that it is possible because I have seen it repeatedly. Both chopsticks are held between the thumb and first finger of the right hand only, and are somehow guided by the other fingers.

The only thing which I thought extraordinary after seeing them consume some eggs in this way was, that the gentleman who had scraped the rind off the outside of the sago plant with his nails, had not done it with his chopsticks.

It would be easy enough to devour rice as Chinamen do, for they merely tipped up the small bowl which contained the rice till it was about on the level of a cup of tea being poured into the mouth. Then they shovelled it in with chopsticks, just as we shovel coals into a furnace.

They were great at making tea, apparently the weakest possible tea, without sugar and of course without milk. They poured it out into little bits of handleless cups, and sipped it as if it were port wine. Four of these little Chinese cups were put on a very small tray. They used such an absurdly small tea-pot that we could not help laughing as we saw them with awfully grave faces pouring out and drinking this very feeble, and one would think very tasteless, beverage.

One of our Chinese fellow-passengers was sick with an overwhelming headache, so he got another Chinaman to pinch him on the chest till it bled. Then he seemed satisfied. Although his head did not get any better, still his soul sat easier.

The Chinese certainly at present seem unspoilt by European innovation. When we were in Singapore I saw a Chinaman cleaning the mudspots off a bright blue umbrella. He produced a bottle full of water, and after sucking this liquid into his mouth, kept shooting it out again over the spotted umbrella till all the mud was washed clean off. A Chinaman has the power of squirting from his mouth harder than any other human being on the face of this vast globe.

CHAPTER XVII

ARRIVAL AT SANDAKAN

AFTER being four days at sea we came in sight of Borneo. There was nothing to see here except hills and mountains, all covered with impenetrable jungle and ever topped in clouds.

Borneo is one of the largest islands in the world. One of its mountain peaks goes wandering up thirteen thousand odd feet into the sky.

We anchored eventually off Labuan, which is an interesting little island about six miles from the main coast.

This, unlike North Borneo or Sarawak, is a little British colony.

I will endeavour to tell you more about Labuan on my return journey, but now let us proceed to Borneo.

When the 'Rance' had amassed all the coal and bananas that she could collect during a stay of thirty hours, we steamed on to a small place with about three houses in it, called Gaya. It is situated on a steep island, quite close to the main Bornean coast, and belongs to the British North Borneo Company. I believe it is sixty miles from Labuan.

Here we were very kindly treated by one Wheatley, the Government agent, who showed us all kinds of curious swords and implements collected from the natives.

Amongst other things was a stuffed crocodile. Then one of us said, 'Now that is a most interesting and amusing creature, and how delightful his teeth look, when he is stuffed like that. A fellow whom I know had a tame one, near whose tank he lived, and he loved it with an appalling affection. One morning when he woke up from a most peaceful and gratifying slumber, he found this crocodile crouching on the end of his bed. Then he gave one fearful yell, and tearing his hair, rushed shrieking from the room. Thus he parted company with that bally alligator for ever.' This story might have been true, or it might have been untrue, but we could scarcely believe it, as we thought that crocodiles, however tame, would not come out of the water into one's bedroom.

This Government agent lived perched up on a hill in a roomy palm-leafed bungalow supported on posts, so that the floor came about eight feet from the light yellow clay soil. Then down below us was the wooden pier, with more palm-leaved houses at its seaward end.

Then we went steaming on past Kina Balu, 13,698 feet high, which is the highest mountain in Borneo; and although we were forty miles from it, still it looked very fine as we got a peep of its lofty summit away amongst the clouds. After this we came to a place called Kudat, where we had to wait thirty-six hours. We were obliged to stay a long time in each of these ports, because the natives and Chinamen would not work after dark; besides which our emigrants would have deserted if we had lain alongside the pier, consequently we were forced to go out about a mile to sea every night. We were going to traverse a difficult part of the coast on the morrow, which it was necessary to take in the daylight, therefore we stopped two nights off Kudat. This, like the other villages along the coast, seemed a brand new little place, quite full of Chinese houses down beside the sea, whilst the natives lived in separate villages out

THE PIER AT KUDAT

on the waters; then away up on the hill, about fifty feet above us, there were two or three European houses, and that was all. My photograph was taken from the ship, when we were slowly nearing the pier, between the coral reefs.

The following day we passed some low-lying islands; on the shores of one called Banguey,[1] I was

[1] Banguey island is the only part of North Borneo which is said to have been of volcanic origin.

told there were two tobacco estates, but these were not apparent to the naked eye as we steamed past, nor were they visible if one clothed one's eyes with glasses, for that matter. What a desolate place this would be to pass one's existence in, with nothing but an untrustworthy steam launch, in which to cross over the many miles of open ocean before reaching civilisation! It is a healthy climate away here on these wooded islands, but how awfully deserted you must feel when you look forth over an endless stretch of ocean! How you must long to see one ship, one boat, one anything, instead of the monotonous distance of sea, only sea! A sea out of whose blue waters fish were constantly jumping, and above whose white coral reefs great eagles hovered, and an innumerable number of birds winged their unceasing way, but still a sea on whose surface no fisherman's boat could be seen. How deserted, how lonely this ocean looked, from our human point of view!

There was a young gentleman who came on board the vessel at Kudat, and was only going with us as far as Sandakan. I forget what his name was, but let us call him 'Silly Infant,' as he would talk, talk unflaggingly till 'all was blue.' Even during this short period, he was so overflowing with animal spirits and information, that it would have been impossible for a second spokesman to squeeze in a word by the edge. He talked incessantly till 12.15 at night, and as we all had our beds on deck and slept on the skylight, it was impossible to do anything but doze while this conversation continued. At 5.30 next morning, however, he awoke, remarking, 'Let me see, I was just telling you about,' etc. etc., and went on as though he had not been interrupted by five and a quarter hours' sleep. Even our captain, who was not only the best of fellows, but the most chatty, absolutely could not get in a word edgeways against this irrepressible young man, who always carried the day.

When we at length arrived at Sandakan—which, by the way, is pronounced Sndārkan—we found ourselves beneath a little bit of a shed at the end of the pier, under the following very interesting circumstances. It was raining in a tropical downpour—so hard, in fact, that it was difficult to hear what your neighbours said to you, as the drops of rain made so much noise coming down on the iron roof. Being nine o'clock at night, it was of course pitch dark. All the coolies had gone away, as their day's work was done. We had left our ship about a mile off, out in the bay, and had what seemed another mile to traverse, from the pier to the house whither we were bound.

At present there are no roads of any sort in Sandakan, the capital of British North Borneo; only yellow clayey footpaths zigzagging up the hills, and sandy tracks along the seashore, where all the natives and Chinamen live. No wheeled vehicle has yet been started in North Borneo, as the roads are not broad enough; even the jinrickshaw is at present unknown. There were a few riding ponies in the town, so that, except your feet, this was the only means of locomotion.

The hotel was a small wooden structure, containing about a dozen bedrooms and *a bar*. We were told it was doubtful whether we could get anything here, fit to eat or not.

After waiting impatiently for three-quarters of an hour the rain cleared off and we were able to get away; but the foot-paths were wet and very slippery, as no stones were used in Sandakan for road mending, and wherever there happened to be a morsel of clay it became quite greasy on a night such as this.

However, at last we reached a large square two-storeyed bungalow, whence the dulcet strains of an English comic song were wafted to us on the hot wet April air.

Sandakan is a very jolly little place, because it is at present so very original. It extends altogether about two and a half miles along the shores of Sandakan Bay. This bay is a great and deep inlet of the sea, being about one mile and a quarter across opposite the steep island of Bahala at the entrance to the bay, and about fifteen miles in length. All the land on the Sandakan side of the harbour is steepish sandstone and sandy land, I believe of the Devonian period. On the opposite side of the bay it is altogether flat, and was probably formed by the mighty Keenabatangan river flowing into the sea, leaving deposit after deposit of light alluvial soil for generations. Therefore from the town you see about four miles away innumerable mangrove swamps coming into the sea and stretching back for many miles inland, till your eye encounters higher ground where ordinary jungle exists.

When I say that Sandakan is about two and a half miles in length, I mean the China town and the two 'campongs' or villages on either side of it, including the saw mills, which occupy a good deal of space. The English residents live scattered about on the hills, within half a mile of the back of the town; some in wooden bungalows, and others in native houses made of poles and palm leaves. Down by the side of the sea there was such an exceedingly strong smell at low tide, of a mixture of Chinamen and bad fish, that on a hot afternoon it was difficult to bear up under its influence. The company who own North Borneo are now busy trying to do away with this aroma, by selling the muddy shore to anyone who is willing to lay down stones and build above low water mark. As the land is very valuable this may be completed in the course of some *years*, but not now— no, not now.

Immediately behind the China town come hills on this natural promontory, a promontory to which I do not think any name has yet been given; hills which are more than half jungle covered, with here and there an Englishman's bungalow surrounded by patches of primeval forest. Here there is an endless maze of green and brown all mixed together, and towering aloft. Even down below, where the jungle has fallen to the fell axe of civilisation, the second growth is beautiful, with large-leaved 'hamerangs' amid a bed of tropical brake-ferns.

When we had been in Sandakan only one day, the weather became brilliantly fine, with a gentle north-easterly wind a-blowing; so that we enjoyed our life after being cooped up in steamers on the ocean, or shut up in the tropical heat of Singapore. There was a certain freedom about life in Sandakan which we found delightful; for instance, the chickens, of which our hostess kept dozens, were so tame that they were constantly coming into the dining-room when we were at breakfast or dinner. The servants could scarcely move about between these birds and the table, without now and again tripping over a feeding fowl. One day I found that through some foolishness I had left my bedroom door open, and a small number of these birds —sixteen I think it was—were under my bed and *on* it.

But this was not the only Bornean creature which made its presence felt in Sandakan, as the spiders were numerous and almost fierce in their attentions to man. Now if there is a thing in this world which I think lucky, it is the gentle adulation of a spider; but when a great hairy fellow comes down from the ceiling by means of a thread as thick as a piece of cotton, and after looking around for a while, twinkles his black eyes and makes a spring for your arm, well of course one does not mind it. But when one of these fellows took it into his enormous head to besprawl himself all over my scalp, this seemed to me to be too bad, as it was encroaching on the kindliness of my disposition. Consequently, when he placed himself in this situation it was more than even my long-suffering gentleness could stand; disgusted I shook him off. At first he ran a little way from me, then stopping and turning round, he seemed to lisp one silent prayer for vengeance on my head. Then he made off rapidly into the verandah's dim twilight outside my door. I felt that a day would come when he would have his revenge.

There were some Chinese geese here which tickled me a good deal by the way that they conducted themselves. I do not know if geese carry on the same games in other countries as they do out here; I have never had the advantage of watching geese so minutely in my own country as I have in this tropical clime. Imagine the folly of going to sleep in broad daylight, when there is the whole night in which I should hope every bird, except an owl, did sleep; and going to sleep on one leg, probably in order to rest the other. There were two Chinese geese asleep at nine o'clock one morning, when I happened to pass by a crowd of these birds. They were geese who generally paddled about all day in a stream below a Chinaman's house in this town. They drowsed quietly on, in spite of the dogs and men who kept passing over the wooden planking of a bridge hard by, with their heads tucked back over one wing, while their beaks were resting beneath the sheltering grasp of the other wing.

I thought what strangely weird birds these were.

There were nine geese altogether; two had their bills shrouded with a covering wing while they slept on one leg. The other seven were standing about, occasionally shaking their feathers thoughtfully in the shallow water in a restful condition, or standing on the sandy bank apparently relishing the soiled leaves of some very dirty grass, at which they kept pecking, and now and again calling in shrill overstrained whispers to one another. Presently a great Chinese dog came down amongst them. Then they seemed offended, and stood perfectly straight up with their heads, necks, and bodies all in a line. Now they waddled very slowly across some green grass close to the stream, all this time making as they swayed forward the most fearful goosish noise to which human ear has ever been a prey. Then two of them slowly flapped their extended wings, and the unoffending dog having by this time moved off, they stood perfectly motionless, left off screaming, and closed their eyes, whether from a feeling of disdain towards the outer world, or because they wished to ease their eyes after using them for this time or two, I could not make out. Here I left them, as I was unable to remain all day watching their movements. It seems to me that geese will be geese everywhere, and certainly these geese were the most awful geese that I had ever seen.

CHAPTER XVIII

WE START FOR THE WILDS

NEARLY seventy-five miles from Sandakan by sea there was a tract of jungle land about 15,000 acres in extent, which had been bought from the North Borneo Company to plant with tobacco. At the time I speak of only six acres of this land had been felled, and none of it planted, but the manager was busy 'burning off' the six acres of felled land.

To this property, which lay on the Toongood River, we intended to go as soon as we could get a 'tonkang,' or native barge, ready to take up a quantity of sawn boards for the construction of a new bungalow which the manager was building on the new estate.

The Toongood River is a branch of the Labuk.[1] On the latter stream there were already two tobacco estates, which had been worked for over a year. Each of these properties had a steam launch, which was kept running to Sandakan about once in ten days.

One of these steam launches came in to Sandakan while we were there. We therefore wrote a very civil letter to the agents, telling them exactly how we were situated, and asking if they could delay her departure for the Labuk four hours, till we could get our tonkang ready, as we wanted to be towed up to the junc-

[1] See the map at the end of the book.

tion of the two rivers, which was only about five miles from the jungle property where we were going. To this civil letter we had a less civil answer, saying that the steam launch would not wait a moment after the specified time. We therefore went to the native captain, and talked the matter over with him. He said he had a relation who was dying, and, as far as we could make out, he would not leave him till he *was* dead. Long before this aged gentleman had breathed his last we had our tonkang ready and lashed to the pier.

The bottom of this barge was full of boards, and on the top of them came our luggage, cook, servants, and ourselves, with an awning over all.

When the moon was shining brightly at about half-past ten at night, the steam launch started off, towing two heavily laden tonkangs behind her; one of these belonged to the owner of the launch, whilst we were on board the other. It was fortunately a dead calm, otherwise we should not have been able to proceed so smoothly over the tropical sea, as the tonkang is an exceedingly bad sea boat, being merely an open barge-shaped construction, about thirty feet long and twelve feet broad. It took us altogether forty-six hours to accomplish that seventy-five miles of sea and river. Our slow progress, however, told hardly on a young Englishman called 'Mum,' who was going up the Labuk to one of the tobacco plantations. The night *before* we started he went aboard the little steam launch with only enough sardines and bread to last him for four meals, thinking that on the following morning at six o'clock the launch would put out to sea with one light tonkang behind her, and would soon

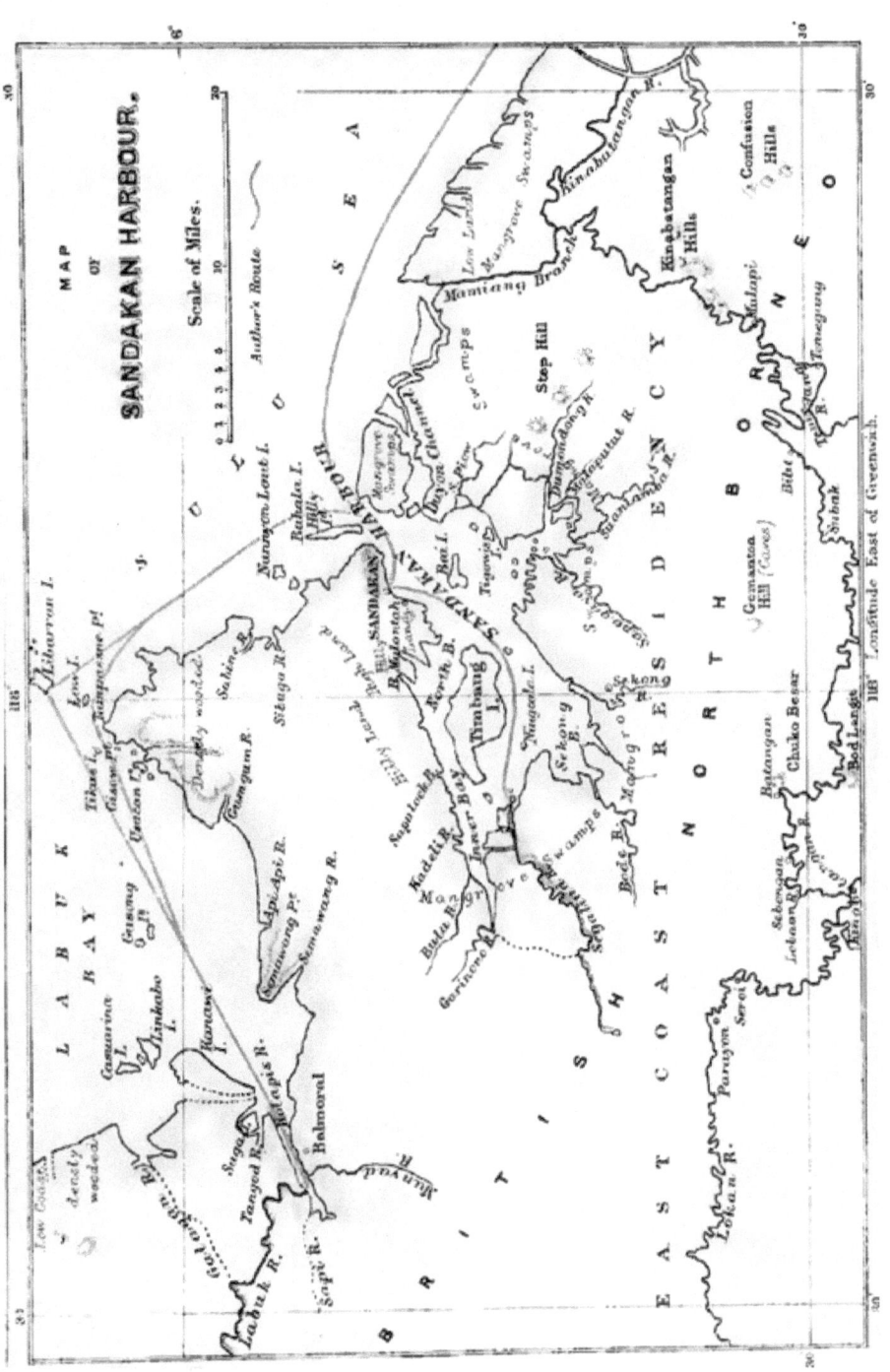

reach the estate; whereas she did not leave Sandakan till the following evening with two heavy tonkangs in tow, so that he not only had a very uncomfortable night lopping about in the harbour on the flattest of hard benches, but, fearing lest she should sail any time during the following day, he stopped aboard wearing his soul out in that square box which I suppose you would call a cabin.

When we steamed out we found the rudder of our tonkang had not been properly shipped. This became very apparent, as she would not steer at all; therefore the captain of the launch had to shut off steam, while we sent two men overboard to try and right it. In doing this we drifted so much that we came right athwart the anchor rope of a native craft which was resting there. This rope became mixed up with our rudder in such a labyrinth of confusion, that after a while our men seemed to find it difficult to tell even which was hemp rope and which was rudder. We were therefore obliged to tell them—unbeknownst to the natives aboard that little sailing ship—to cut this anchor rope and let our rudder go free. This was promptly done, and then we got away.

We supposed that when the natives found out their drifting condition, they must have made the gentle moonlight *pale* before their execrations, but we did not hear them, as the thud, thud of our little steamer was all that was borne to our ears over the subdued water.

We soon left Pulo Bay Island behind, with its low-lying tropical trees, and the many miles of flat looking mangrove swamps on the opposite shore to Sandakan. After a while we saw by the full moonlight that we were getting right out into the ocean as we steamed slowly round the intervening headlands of Bahala, and away to the dark blue distance beyond.

All the next morning we were crossing more sun-lit seas, but now the distance was hidden by treey islands. By four o'clock we had got amongst swamps again in the mangroved entrance of the Labuk river. We stopped for half an hour off a forest-covered hill, which had been christened Balmoral out of respect for our Queen. It was a very poor place, with only five or six native huts or piles coming out of the river.

That night we anchored for about six hours, as there is a certain danger to boats travelling at night on account of the 'snags.' Great mangrove trees, looking like birch trees at home, were all around us, and these mingled with the nepah's feathery palm leaves, were all that we could see from the flat river's bed.

The next morning we got into a straggling native village, not closely packed, but with huts about every hundred yards apart, and with boats constantly flitting from one side to the other. These houses were all nepah-covered, with sloping concave roofs, and each house had an entrance from the river—an entrance made of very broad ladders from the water up to the doors of the houses. The houses were altogether built on piles driven into the muddy banks, as these people make the river their highway, and have no paths and no connection with one another inland. There were a few native ladies in front of the houses, and any number of jolly little children bathing and amusing themselves as much in the water as out of it.

It was towards noon on the second day that we at length approached the first of the three so-called tobacco plantations in this part of Borneo. In two of them the nursery stage seemed only to have been reached; nevertheless they were called tobacco estates.

Here the launch left us, as it was bound for a property further up the main river. The jungle to which we were going, as I said before, was situated about five miles up a branch of the Labuk.

The manager of the property was soon made acquainted with our arrival, and immediately set out in a boat to collect his visitors. By nine o'clock that night we were up at his bungalow, enjoying the rice and chickens which he had provided for our reception.

The last ten miles of our trip had been entirely through jungle, except where a Dutchman had felled about 300 acres in readiness for planting tobacco.

After winding our way up the stream we had at length seen flames, caused by the burning of felled forest; flames from the only six acres of cleared land on this estate, thus leaving 14,994 acres of standing jungle on the property.

This jungle was so thick that man could not penetrate it at will. It only seemed to be frequented by innumerable monkeys and butterflies of every hue and size, which made the forest bright with their lazy wings.

This uncivilised country is peopled with monkeys. You can scarcely go round the bend of any river without seeing monkeys high up above decamping along the branches of the trees. If you are walking they very often remain motionless till you get right beneath the lofty boughs to which they are clinging; then the playful crowd will all rush off together, making such a disturbance that you cannot help thinking the old gentleman himself must have got into the lonely jungle.

We saw one orang-utan in the forest; and at Kudat the Government agent had two great big ones who were tame; at least, we were told they were *quite* tame, but they did not look inviting, so we did not try. They were tied to trees in his garden. We were informed that they were only very playful amongst themselves, which we were glad of.

CHAPTER XIX

IN THE LOW-LYING TOBACCO COUNTRY

ALL the low-lying land in British North Borneo is covered with almost impenetrable jungle. It is so thickly covered with timber and scrub, that there is scarcely an acre in the flat country where you can penetrate without some native going before you to cut the way. This makes travelling amongst the tangled mass of foliage and creepers a heavy and laborious task.

It is anything but healthy on the swampy land of this primeval forest. Being only raised a few feet above the sea level, it is flooded every year during the rainy season. The climate is therefore decidedly damp.

There is, I believe, a rainfall of nearly two hundred inches in the year, consequently the wash coming off the mountains must be very great. The flat lands of North Borneo have been completely formed by generations of wash coming down in this way, and leaving a very recent deposit.

It is most difficult for new-comers to get any drinkable water. Of course this is one of the reasons why there is so much fever among the Europeans and a disease called 'bery-bery' amongst the imported labour. Some of the new tobacco estates are particularly unhealthy, not only on account of the water, but all land when it is first opened so near the equator must be unwholesome with the tropical sun and rain coming down on freshly dug up earth and decaying vegetation.

I think that all young men who go out to a country like this ought to make some provision before leaving home by which they can get back again if necessary. What can a young Dutch fellow do on a tobacco estate in North Borneo, when he has come all these miles across the sea, buoyed up with the hope of eventually becoming rich, as many of the planters in Sumatra have already done, when he finds at the outset that, in spite of his dogged determination to get on, his health is failing him, and he has not the money to take him back to a European climate?

When a tobacco estate has been opened a year or two, and the manager's bungalow is placed on land which has been formerly cultivated, it becomes infinitely more wholesome and healthy.

The Chinese coolies who are opening an estate sometimes die off like rats. This happens on all the properties situated in an unwholesome part of the country. A Dutch planter said to me, talking of the estate on which he was then living, 'This place is wonderfully healthy: we have only had thirty coolies die within the last month.' 'Out of how many?' I asked. 'Well, out of 220; whereas look at such and such a place on the Keenabatangan, where 150 have died out of 300 in the month.'

I was told that the Chinese coolies could live healthily near Deli, in the great tobacco country of Sumatra, all the days of their existence. Probably they will be able to live in the same way here in a few years' time, but at present, owing to the unhealthiness of opening estates amid the interminable jungle, and the class of opium-smoking coolies who are obtained from Singapore, the death-rate is terribly high.

The most successful tobacco planters seem to be those who have been engaged in the same occupation in Sumatra, before coming to Borneo, as from what I could understand the low country about Deli has much the same climate as North Borneo.

It is difficult to imagine how some of these tobacco estates will pay when they are worked by English or Scotch men, who have had scarcely any training or experience in the cultivation of tobacco, considering the estates have to pay as much as 100 dollars (nearly 17*l.*) for each coolie. At present the Chinese coolie can be imported to Deli, in Sumatra, at infinitely less cost than here, although the distance from Swatow, in China, must be nearly double what it is from Swatow to Sandakan. But the planters there have steamers running for no other purpose than carrying coolies.

North Borneo possesses at any rate one advantage over Sumatra—viz., land can be bought here now for an almost *nominal* sum. As in all new countries, the planter has a good deal to contend with at first. There are no Government cart roads in the country yet, and the seaway is the only means of transport. It is true that this seaway is very remarkable, as one can get a great many miles up most of the tidal rivers, in the low-lying country, by means of a steam launch. It is only possible to penetrate the low lands, and of course one cannot tell what is in the interior, or what the soil and rainfall may be away on those mountain sides which were discernible from the sea.

There seems little doubt that many paying productions might be grown, if only one could get cheaper labour; labour which might be imported from India or the Straits Settlements.

The soil here appeared very rich, if one could judge from the magnificent jungle and rich undergrowth.

It is not a good sporting country, although there is plenty of game; but the jungle is so filled up with undergrowth, and in places so crowded with an impenetrable bamboo, that it makes silent walking after game very difficult.

I was told that in the flat lands, which extend from twelve to fifteen miles into the interior, there was not a single acre of open country, all this recent deposit being terribly overgrown.

About the bison and elephant of North Borneo I shall have something to say later on. There are in all four different kinds of big game to be shot out here: the elephant, the bison, the rhinoceros, and the deer. I do not consider wild-tame buffalo to be game.

CHAPTER XX

BOS BANTENG

We had come here to shoot, so let me describe our first day's shooting adventure.

My friend had brought four Javanese men with him from Batavia, three of whom always accompanied us on our jaunts in the jungle. Two of these men were old gun-bearers, who could follow up marvellously the fresh trail of any animal, and could detect the objects of the chase in the thickest forest long before the ordinary Englishman discerned anything but a tangled mass of leaves.

Besides these men, we took with us a little Javanese servant, who carried a huge vulcanite bottle full of cold tea. This bottle was encased in felt, and was constantly dipped in any muddy jungle water that we passed, thereby rendering the tea inside deliciously cool and refreshing.

In Borneo you live on boiled rice—this is your staple food; the natives eat nothing else, and I believe it is wholesome, although of all dry tasteless foods commend me to simple rice without curry or milk. We always took with us a packet of rice, tied up with bark strings in two large green leaves which the natives use instead of paper. This was not our only form of food, as we consumed therewith a sort of long, lonely, raw ham-sausage, made in Holland, which was much too salt for my taste in cold blood. Also, having British prejudices, I did not like uncooked ham.

We soon got into the swampy jungle, where a tree called rizophore threw out innumerable roots. Roots that made one swear, as they seemed to have grown simply to annoy the harmless traveller. Roots with pointed angles coming up all over the ground about one foot high, then going down into the ground again in the shape of a capital $\mathcal{M}$. They were just hard enough to provoke you to tread on them, but not sufficiently stable to bear the whole weight of your body. I thought that if anything deserved a bad name, it was these deceptive wooden angles. Please remember, when I say they were 'most damnable,' that when I encountered them I was rather tired and very hot. I should think, from their shape, that this ground must have been under water for six months in the year.

When I speak of rizophore swamps, I do not mean that there was nothing else besides this tree, as there was a thick undergrowth everywhere. We also saw a great quantity of objects most interesting to the human eye. Amongst other trifles we were fascinated by the appearance of two sorts of fungi, growing far away from the haunts of men. One of them had a white stem—as most fungi have—from the top of which, about thirteen inches from the ground, there came down a cage of white honeycombed network, making an enclosure large enough for a canary's cage. On the top of the central stem there was a light green knob.

If this fungus sounds too extraordinary to be true, I must refer my readers to the backwoods of a Bornean jungle, where they can go and see it for themselves. If all Oriental mushrooms smell as strongly as this one did, I pity anyone who indulges in picking them.

There was another kind of fungus which struck me as being very peculiar, for it grew on a tall dead-black stem. The specimen we came across was about one foot two inches high, then came a perfectly black dish surrounded by a broad white rim.

We also passed quantities of pitcher-plants, some growing on stems by themselves, others at the end of a fern leaf like a long oval hart's-tongue.

We came across several little mounds which were rendered beautiful by the numerous Neboung palms. It seemed as if no other trees would grow amongst these palms, since they absorb all the good, even of the poorest soil. From this tree the natives slice out supple pieces of wood for tying on to the sides of houses to keep the dry palm-leaves in place.

Then there was a vast acreage of flat land covered with very much overgrown forest, and in this flat land the bison (*Bos Banteng*) disports himself all through the day, only at night going down to the river to drink.

The Bornean bison is one of the largest wild bison that exists anywhere in the world. This particular species is, I think, found only on Barli Island, in Java, and Borneo. I believe that it belongs to the same genus as the *Bos Gaurus*, the only perceptible difference being that, though the bulls of both the Banteng and the Gaurus are black with white

M

stockings, still the cow of the Banteng is a deep reddish brown, while the Gaurus cows are black. They are utterly different from the Tsine of Burmah, which, I am told, is only a tame Bos genus which has for many years run wild. They are something the shape of the domestic cow, with a hump on their backs, and a drop in front of it of from four and a half to five inches. But their height is enormous compared with our shorthorns at home. The bull of this species stands about six feet two inches high at the shoulder. In spite of his height, he is most difficult to discern when at rest or feeding in the thick forest.

About eleven o'clock on our first day we came across quite fresh tracks, which made us sure that the game could not be far ahead. After following these for about an hour, dodging and scrambling pretty silently amid the growing labyrinth, Van, who had won the toss in the morning, came in sight of some bison feeding about forty yards away. He put up his rifle to have a shot, but at this moment the ugliest of our Javanese gun-bearers, who had been suffering from a cough lately, gave way to a hacking bark, which you would have said was anything but human. These bison, however, took it for a strange sound issuing from some unknown beast—in which particular they were right—so that they promptly decamped, and Van was left silently and gently muttering oaths.

We thought, however, that never having heard a human being before, they would not go very far, and in this we were right. We had not proceeded on their tracks more than half a mile before we came up with them again. On this occasion Van merely fired at something brown, which he could see in the distance amidst a crowd of jungle leaves, as he feared that if he approached nearer, they might be scared. Then one rifle shot sounded in the stillness, and the bison lay struggling on the ground, shot through the back-bone.

We had about two miles to accomplish before getting home. We always carried compasses with us, as without them one would be lost, unless the sun was shining and either rising or falling. We then steered for the river along which was a track. The ugliest of our Javanese went before us to cut down the undergrowth the whole way with a Javanese knife. This knife was a cut between a sword and a very long-bladed bill-hook, and was worn in a scabbard.

When we got back to the estate—I was going to say to 'the plantation,' but I suppose I should err in calling the six acres of felled jungle 'a plantation'— we sent out twelve coolies to bring in portions of the defunct corpse, which they did with the greatest alacrity. This was a delightful change to them after hacking up the berooted land round the bungalow. Besides which they all got some of the meat, and for comestible purposes it proved a first-rate old cow of the jungle.

CHAPTER XXI

SOME BORNEAN NATIVES

ALTHOUGH we were twenty miles from the mouth of the river, a certain rise and fall of the tide made itself felt, and this was also the case in a slighter degree two miles further up the Toongood; but there it ended. In spite of our being under this tidal influence, there were quantities of fish both large and small in the stream. But having omitted to bring a fly rod from Europe with us, we could not entangle them, although we angled with the utmost assiduity. We fished with rice and with the fruit of a jungle tree which grew over the river. Small pieces of this fruit were constantly cast into the sluggish stream by the monkeys, so that fish were always rising beneath the boughs, and snatching at morsels which fell on the shining water.

I noticed five different kinds of fresh-water fish in the blue depths of this silent river. There was a very small fish something like a stickleback. Another about the same shape and size as a gudgeon, and quantities of fish very much like the roach, only with rather larger scales. Also a great big fish weighing up to about six or eight pounds, with a perfectly smooth, scaleless skin, and two limp porcupine-looking quills coming away from its jaw, and reaching down to the tail. What the use of these protuberances may be, I am quite at a loss to imagine. The natives generally use an animal like a big cray-fish, which they manage to attract from its hole among the sandstone rocks, as a bait. These large fish are marked very funnily; they are a lightish colour all over the body, with four oval black spots *down* their sides, and red tips to their tails.

There is yet another fish about six inches in length, which appears to swim entirely with its tail, as it goes wagging itself up and down with short jerks. This species has the most startlingly projecting black eyes, surrounded by a circle of white. Its body is covered with broad black spots on a greenish white background. In fact, this is the most showy fish we saw in tropical waters.

I hope that someone will write a book, one of these days, about the fish in North Borneo and how to catch them otherwise than with dynamite, as this seems nearly the only method now in vogue amongst Europeans.

Apropos of fishing, an Englishman who had been staying up the Trusan River, which runs out in Brunei Bay, told me the following:

'The natives had been for some weeks collecting "tuber" from the forest and depositing it in bundles under the fort where we were staying. Tuber is said to be a creeper, and not plentiful. The root, which is used for fishing purposes, has a heavy sweet odour something like bignonia flowers.

'The fishing began on a day when the water was very low and clear: it took place in a part of the river which was free from rapids. They beat the tuber out, filling the bottoms of their canoes with a milky fluid which exuded from the roots.

'A short time after they had capsized their canoes fish came to the surface and gasped, *apparently* to suck in air, but a slight touch was enough to make them dart off. Then the natives speared the larger ones and caught the smaller ones with nets.'

The trees were very beautiful all the way up the river, especially a kind of ficus, or banyan, which was perpetually dropping its fruit into the water. This is the tree beneath whose shade were a crowd of ever-rising fish. The leaves on these trees are exceedingly small and green, but they have white, or almost white, stems and bark.

The tree-ferns, hanging down in great solid balls of root over the water, were indeed strange. One wonders how they came there, so far away from the ground, apparently growing on nothing; really they are lodged on the minute stems of creepers. This fern looks like a very large and green hart's-tongue, and I believe it is called the large elk's-horn. In this way it grows on a thread, balancing itself between us mortals on this hot earth and heaven's blue vault above.

At a certain season of the year it is incased in a most beautiful pot of green foliage. From this pot descend a great quantity of offshoots, so that this enormous fern has what I should call three sorts of leaves: the hart's-tongue fern-leaves, the pot which is something like the outside of a cabbage, and the drooping tendrils resembling nothing that I ever saw before in my life, except perhaps pieces of thick penny-a-yard green ribbon.

On this estate they were building a new house

down by the sad pools of that jungle-reflecting river, instead of the iniquitous mosquitoey place where we were then living. It was being constructed almost entirely without nails. The natives sew the beams together with long strips of rattan which have been cut out on purpose, as the British nail is almost unused here.

Native tools are generally employed, and it is very

OUR BUNGALOW IN BORNEO

extraordinary in this age to come across a part of the country where the American axe is an almost unknown weight. Except the boy who cuts up kindling at my English home, and who uses an old-fashioned piece of iron with a straight stem for an axe, I had thought that our cousin's implements were used everywhere; however, it seems that I was wrong, as the coolies on this estate had not come up to the Yankee invention yet.

The insects in our dining-room were in such countless thousands that they would indeed scandalise the English housewife. On the table during the daytime hundreds of little ants, which you could scarcely follow with your eye in their quick gyrations from one side to the other, were always on the move, looking out for morsels of sugar, or anything edible which might be left after our meal. They also eat the remains of a small sort of cockroach, of which in a week we killed hundreds. These creeping animals would always crawl over our books or our paper when we were reading.

After dark, however, the ants were not so troublesome, but flying insects which constantly flitted around the lamp were then the predominating nuisance. For instance, flying ants, cockroaches, beetles, moths and grasshoppers were everywhere. I do not speak of the 'Praying Mantis.' The largest and brightest green varieties were constantly getting mixed up between one's mouth and cigar end, and entangling themselves in one's hands. The white lamp became perfectly black every evening with dying flying insects, whose legs and wings had become transfixed in the stickiness of its paraffiny surface.

There was also a beast that we dreaded because he was so assiduously rough-and-tumble in his persevering attention to man. This was the 'Tongered' (Malay), 'Cicada' (Latin). He came in the stillest hours of evening, when we were just thanking our stars that the cool night was at length settling down after a day of perspiration, probably after a day of search for jungle beasts which we never found.

The days in this tropical heat were very tiring,

although we might have been dressed in almost nothingness—viz., a thin linen jacket and trousers made by the Chinese, which were wonderfully light in texture. Still the exercise was exceedingly wearing work, and we came home worn out with our toil. Then it was very tiresome to have a huge ungainly brute, about two and a half inches long—with large unblinking eyes that frightened you—come bouncing in and whirling round and round in the most unblushing way. It would stop perfectly motionless for two seconds, only that it might have breath to go on again; when this had continued for about half an hour we felt quite crazed with prolonged agony, and saw that the only path to peace was to get behind the mosquito curtains. Having extinguished the lights, sleep at length came

THE 'TONGERED'

to our wearied eyelids, and we were for a time out of this exasperating misery—out of the hell on earth into which these interesting animals had made our bungalow.

I will try and give you some idea from my journal of how I was situated in the evenings: 'It is evening now; the clock marks half-past seven. We have been out stalking, and have returned wet and weary. We have had our dinner off chicken soup and Hong Kong potatoes, chicken bones and potatoes, finishing up with unedible salt beef and potatoes. The lamp before me is already quite black with dead winged insects; I have just counted sixteen to the square inch. Huge sort of earwigs are crawling about the table at which I am writing, to say nothing of flying ants, and night-flies of an emerald green with pink eyes. Small creeping beetles are also there, and in spite of my having my trousers tucked into my socks, there are—yes, there certainly are—insects creeping up my legs, as the floor is also covered with living creatures. One fly that I have just slain is quite beautiful; it has a body the colour of pink blotting-paper, and imagination defies one to dream of such fairy wings, such pink transparent wings, with a creamy coloured boundary all round.

'On the table beyond this is a well-known novel by Charles Lever, a pair of nail scissors, a bottle half-full of some iniquitous compound which they call claret, and two earthenware jars filled with the most doubtful filtered water. Then comes a long Chinese cane-bottomed chair, in which Van is smoking Sumatran cigars, reading a novel between whiles when these myriads of insects will let him. Next there is a sideboard, made by the natives out here without nails; its timbers are tied together with pieces of bamboo, on which every ant in the universe seems to be collected, trying to attack certain jams which are placed in basins of water to keep them at bay.

'Beyond that is the darkness of night, and about ten yards away is the jungle, whence comes a chorus from thousands of crickets. One cricket constantly gives a lullaby sound, while another is like the distant barking of a very high-voiced terrier. Some are just singing, others chirping, so that the medley which is borne to us from the primeval forest hard by, is mingled together in a multiplication of harmony, conducive to sleep if to nothing else. Out here, when we have been walking in this hot dense jungle for six hours at a stretch, sleep comes to our wearied bodies uncourted and almost unsought.'

Many miles from the sea as we were, the days were hotter than they were down by the shore, but the night watches were certainly cooler. When darkness had come in its sudden way over the earth, and we had concluded our meal, we turned in behind the mosquito curtains and were soon slumbering beneath the kajung roof.

One day, whilst staying in this immense tract of hitherto unexplored jungle, we went up the river about five miles, till we saw a hill in the distance. We saw this hill because a few acres of land had been felled, where some Dyaks and Doessans had settled. We stopped some time at a place where a quantity of pebbles were left uncovered by the retiring tide. Two boatloads of Dyaks from Sarawak had also unshipped themselves there (the Rajah of Sarawak, you may remember, has his kingdom in Borneo). They lived up this river, and were on their homeward way after an outing to some friendly tribe up another tidal stream. They told us how their tribe had had a battle with some Doessans who lived about six days' journey up the Toongood, and how they had killed some eighty men, when they were only thirty warriors themselves. We believed that there were altogether about a thousand Doessans up the river, but whether they had all joined in doing battle with this warlike little tribe or no we could not tell, so that we only answered in the British tongue, saying: 'Go, tell that to the Marines! We know that you are the most warlike tribe in Borneo, but this killing business is a thing that we *cannot* believe.' Then we resumed the conversation in their language. We thought that these folks had either allowed their imagination to presume very much on past events, or that they were lying to deceive us. They were all fine healthy-looking fellows, tattooed in blue over their hands and bodies with remarkably pretty and artistic patterns, which were all very similar.

The Dyaks appear to suffer from very experienced dentists, as they all have their teeth cut off almost to the gums, and there are crosses of a metal which looks like gold put through each tooth, and this, with their gums running down with betel-nut, makes their appearance fascinating in the extreme.

As it was low tide we went up several little rapids, and eventually got out of tidal waters. Then we paddled through the beautiful tropical jungle to a spot where there were ever so many native houses, each one more dishevelled looking than the last, but with quite well-to-do families 'aboard' them. I use this term as you have to climb up a ladder on to these houses just as you do on to the deck of a ship, as each dwelling was raised four feet, at any rate, on sticks above the ground.

We visited four houses and found the natives quite friendly to the British stranger. They asked us to sit down on their clean mats, in spite of our boots being quite covered with dirt. In one smallish room five families were living, and anything to compare with the shortness, stoutness, and ugliness of the females it would be impossible to find.

In one of the houses which was inhabited by Dyaks they had a very interesting collection of old Chinese cannon. Cannon made literally *years* ago, and brought over here by Chinese pirates. These cannon, which were made of brass or bronze, were covered all over with patterns. Doubtless the time will come when the Dyaks will be so civilised, or so drunken, that they will want to sell them; but at present they would rather part with their souls than these curiosities.

They all had dogs; partially civilised races always seem to have dogs.

There are dogs by the dozen in the islands of Tonga, South Pacific. Dogs by the hundred in Greece, and dogs by the thousand in Constantinople. Some of them are half-starved, and are generally anxious to bite you if they can make up their minds to face the stranger; but, except in the out-of-the-way parts of Greece, they have not the required pluck. In Greece a few years back, and I suppose it is the same now, dogs to the south of the Gulf of Patras were rendered uncommonly fierce by the natives. When passing a native's house, two or three of these yellow-coloured brutes would fly out and lay hold of you, unless you could find stones to keep them at bay. If you shot them the natives seized you, and would not let you go without paying a ransom.

When travelling in a far and foreign country like Borneo, you do not find, as far as my experience goes, the folks who live here half so disagreeable or so dangerous as, for instance, the common Greeks. I am told that in the Solomons, which, I believe, are the only islands in the world where missionaries have failed to penetrate, the natives are either very friendly or else take a dislike to you and kill you right off. How much better this is than in Greece, where they naturally hate every stranger! It is only by putting a veil over their feelings that they become civil, but really they and their great yellow dogs are bullies together.

But to return to the Bornean native dogs. They are smooth-haired and look like little terriers. They seem courteous to the stranger. In the native houses they sit just below you on a sort of floor made of bars of wood, about four feet from the ground. I say a sort of floor, because the dogs which we saw on our visit up the river were just balanced on four crossed sticks; there was nothing beneath them but the earth, with here a goat tending her young or there some chickens feeding and pecking about. Some of these birds were looking wise, and throwing out a remark now and then as hens always will, and the dogs sat snoozing up above them, so mild and gentle in their deportment that it was difficult to believe we were amongst an only partially civilised race.

Then, about one foot above the dogs, came the floor of the native abode, which was an endless transparent matting of sticks woven together with about an inch between each stick, through which you could see the dog, the goat, and the chickens beneath you. It also let in a very delightful air to us, literally sun-bescorched from the river that we had left down below.

The whole ceiling seemed to be composed of an originally brilliant coloured, but now faded, mosquito curtain, made out of thin chintz. This was evidently let down at night over a whole family; thus with their mats they could keep out of their abode all flying things.

The small children were swinging in little beds hanging from the roof. The bar above each little bed was covered with charms, doubtless to soothe the devil and keep him at bay. But they were very funny charms used for this purpose. I saw little bits of chains, chains which out here are attached to a casting-net, just as lead is used at home; and all sorts of things tied in small leaf-made bundles, precious things I should think, which would be sure to scare the old gentleman if he should be around.

The furniture of their house was very simple; it consisted of a few cooking utensils, some logs of bamboo which, I believe, contained rice, an old-fashioned European gun, and about five Dyak swords. There were also the paddles of their canoes, some fish-hooks, lines, and a few mats, and some small bags hung up which might have contained anything.

They seldom cultivate more than half an acre of land, which seems to be laid aside for the production of rice. Fishing and making war upon their enemies suit their fancy more than anything else.

We stayed about watching the natives and trying to talk to them for some time. At length we wended our way homeward, a much easier matter than coming up, as the tide was with us.

CHAPTER XXII

OUR RETURN

One day some natives brought us a large fire-back pheasant that they had caught by some heathen means out in the jungle, and as I have never before seen a pheasant of this sort, I will give you some idea of what it was like.

Its beak was light-coloured; its eyes were the most beautiful magenta; its head was light blue, shiny, and featherless, except on its crown, where there were about twenty quills standing straight up in the air; its body was dark purple all over, except a few inches from the tail, where there came a large spot of velvety red feathers; and its tail had a clump of yellow ochre plumage, surrounded by some feathers which were such a dark blue that they appeared almost black.

The fire-back pheasant is pretty common out here; it always alights on the tops of the tallest trees, where it is difficult to see it. There it utters the following crow all the morning and part of the evening: 'Whoo what———————whoo what————————what ————————what————————whoo————————what———— what————wt————-wt————t——-t——t-t,' beginning very slowly and ending in a terrible hurry.

The natives brought at the same time, thinking, I suppose, that we were in want of *birds* for table purposes, a curious mixture between a bird and a cat, called the flying squirrel.[1] This creature was brown and hairy all over his body, with furry speckles like buttons on his outside, but underneath all brown and covered with very fine hairs. He had the largest and most brilliant eyes of any animal I have ever seen, with short, perky ears which always looked as if they were cocked. He measured one foot five inches from the end of the tail to the tips of the ears. His whole person was covered with loose, hairy skin, which expanded when he extended his legs, and hung down in loose folds when he was walking.

I cannot fancy anything more dreadful than seeing one of these bright-eyed little squirrels flying about one's porch at night, because with their dark brown wings and shadowy outlines they would make one think they were the restless shadow of one's mother-in-law.

I am told there is some doubt about these four-footed animals, whether they can fly up to the height whence they came, or no; as it is believed that they cannot 'flit any,' as the Yankees say. I mean that they cannot use their kite-like skin as wings. The question I believe remains unsettled, if they can rise up from one tree to the same height on another, or, in fact, whether they have the power of motion in their flight.

In the daytime there were always great, big, uncanny-looking birds flying about, which with their top-heavy heads and enormous beaks made one think of an ugly dream. With outstretched necks and scarecrow wings, they flitted hoarsely croaking over our heads, like demons in distress. This was the

[1] This was a specimen of the flying lemur, *Galeopitmecus*.

hornbill, of which I was told there were four different sorts in Borneo. One that we shot was the only bird of any real value, as having a solid horn over its beak; it is worth at least five pounds in Java. The Chinese make buttons from this ivory-looking excrescence.

Now that I have got on the subject of animals, let me proceed to the snake. We found one day, when returning from the jungle, a little snake curled up on the path, sleeping its happy hours away in the sunshine. It was apparently only an innocent little thing with a large pink-and-yellow-coloured check pattern all over its body. We slew that serpent with a great stick, as he was what the Javanese call an 'Olar Lemah,' which happens to be one of the most poisonous snakes in the jungle.

Then on the last day before we left the estate there was an enormous fire made with heaps of branches from the fallen timber, which it was necessary to burn off before tobacco could be planted.

When feeding the flames I saw a very big chameleon of the brightest emerald green, who must have been two feet long, though most of his length was tail. The poor beast seemed to have been startled out of his lair, and out of his senses, by flames which encompassed him on every side. He stood beside me gazing at the light all round, too bewildered even to move, although I kept passing close to him. I hoped that poor chameleon would see a to-morrow, though I doubt if he ever did.

Eventually we left the six acres of clearing and came down the river about nine miles, where we made an encampment on about as lovely a spot as it is possible to imagine. Our tent was a good big one;

it was one of those tropical double tents with an outer tent cloth, so that it was perfectly cool during the heat of the day. We had two canvas beds rigged up inside and a mosquito netting over each.

The tent was placed beneath the forest trees, down beside the river. In looking out over this deep, muddy flowing stream, you saw first of all trees, which rendered the spot shady; trees with great leaves, like

THE BACK OF A DUTCHMAN'S BUNGALOW IN THE LOW COUNTRY ABOUT THIRTY MILES INLAND

overgrown walnut leaves at home, coming down in a fringe almost to the water's edge. Beneath these a sort of black tarpaulin tent had been placed by our men, wherein to sleep. There were gun-cases on the ground, and up above, hanging on slight timber cross-bars under this roof, were the clothes of our four men —I mean their change of clothes.

To the right, a few yards away, was the temporary

kitchen, with a great high table made out of bits of jungle wood, tied together with rattan, as of course the spiked nail was an unknown weight with us. Upon this table were always stowed away more things than could conveniently be put there, so that some chickens which were bought from a passing Doessan's boat, and which were tethered with long bits of rattan to the table legs, found it a most convenient locality, as they were always picking up bits of curry stuffs and rice which the cook let fall. The fire came just beyond this: a fire whose blue smoke against the dark green leaves, reminded me of many a day when bustling scenes have ended with pipes round the careless camp fire in colder climates.

There was to the left an apparently endless mass of a species of wild sugar cane growing right down to the margin of the river, presenting a sombre green-and-yellow background. A rope hung before the tent covered with bath towels, socks, and jerseys put there to dry. The whole was backed up by the primeval forest on the opposite side of the water. It was indeed a beautiful picture to look at once in a way; but when the thought occurred to your mind that it was always the same, day after day and year after year through the endless cycles of eternity, and has been, as Mark Twain says, 'through the twilight of tradition,' it appeared a *trifle* more monotonous than an Englishman with English thoughts could stand.

The flies were just too terrible in this far off jungle land. Flies of every sort came buzzing outside our tent, and into it. We had a table rigged up for comestible purposes, and a bench beneath it; these were the most delightful places in a picture that you can conceive, as the deep shadow of trees hedged them in on all sides. But when you came to real life, there were mosquitoes of course, yes, lots of them, sandflies, and big buzzing black flies that stung whenever they got a chance, which was not infrequently, as they could pitch upon your pants without making the slightest noise; then they wheedled their proboscis in between the stitches, as though there was nothing in the way. You were not aware of their presence until you felt the most horrible sting; even then they seemed all prepared to fly away if you made the slightest movement, or even turned round to see the cause of your misery.

All these were nothing compared with the ants and leeches. The ants climb up the roots of certain trees; this is done without any reason, as far as one can see, except it may be in order to annoy passers by. As we were generally the only persons who had foolishly wandered along that particular piece of jungle since the foundation of Borneo, these creeping insects must have found it rather slow work waiting, ever watching for someone on whom to vent their stinging passions. When they did at length find us they launched out, as our five persons were constantly so covered with revengeful ants, stinging to the best of their ability, that our men, with their bare legs, were very often nearly driven to distraction. They could not put down their knives, because they had to cut a way through the almost impenetrable jungle, and of course could not put down our eight-bore guns which they were carrying in their other hands, so had to endure for a few minutes the nips of these infuriated little beasts.

Then the leeches—but I have already told you enough to make it apparent that life in this low-lying jungle, even in fine weather, is not all bliss. In wet weather not only is it oppressively hot and unhealthy, but you have *all* these plagues a hundredfold worse.

From this camp we saw a very large crocodile swimming up the river, and a great many pigs, one of which we shot. But pigs are useless here, as they dig up and devour defunct Chinamen, so that they fail to come up to our ideas of human food. However, we had one Chinaman with us to look after our boat, who consumed the pig greedily.

After wandering about the forest for two days, looking for bison, we suddenly heard the whistle of a steamer going up the river, and as we knew that this would be our only chance of leaving these aborescent banks for nine days, we were obliged to make signals to her as she was returning, and hasten on board.

When we got down the river, how cool, how delicious, and how fresh the sea seemed after our stay of sixteen days in the Bornean interior! I never *liked* being at sea before, but its flylessness was quite delightful to our irritated natures.

There was one bird on this river which I ought to mention. He was such a peculiar and unorthodox sort of fowl, that his circumstances attracted my attention. His name was, I think, an 'Indian Darter;' our Malay servants called him Monok Besse; he was like so many of the larger Bornean birds, remarkably thin, and appeared as though his food did not agree with him. On his first appearance it was difficult to tell whether he was a bird or not, as he was swimming along *beneath* the water, with nothing above but a snake-like neck and head. This is the way these creatures always sail about, looking infinitely more like serpents than birds. We then got closer to this retiring fowl, who, with a rushing sound and an enormous amount of flutter, rose gradually from the river; he flew across with dripping wings, and seemed to be quite out of his element when flying. I never dreamed of anything more long, stiff, and water-washed than this black dripping object looked. Eventually he pitched on a bush beside the water's edge; he did not appear to have fixed on any particular branch, but just came down haphazard, with all his wet-through wings stretched out, and looked uncomfortable till we got out of sight. Whether he ever collected himself and sat in a more bird-like position we do not know.

Our boat was called the 'Normanhurst,' and was quite a big vessel of sixty tons register, with her deck amidships and before the funnel; she had been hired for the trip by one of the two estates up the Labuk. We had to go out some miles from the mouth to an island called Labaran, where the owner of the estate had left a tonkang collecting sea-weed beneath the sea, which he wished to have brought to the surface again. It took the captain of our ship ten hours to get that boat righted.

The island of Labaran is sandy and flat, and is covered with thin high jungle. We were anchored about three-quarters of a mile away from the coast, but even at that distance we could hear the jungle crickets making such a loud singing all through the middle of the day, that in spite of the sailors pumping, and the engine giving vent to occasional very hoarse breathing, their singing could easily be distinguished across the intervening sea. The weary day was almost closing when we were able to put the tonkang in tow and start off for Sandakan.

Man is but an erring thing, full of fear and all kinds of like sensations when any imaginary cause for such feelings crops up. It is pleasant to think that in your individual case there never was, and never will be, any fear; but just wait until your time comes.

When we got to Sandakan some very black clouds which we had seen over the distant low-lying country came up and overshadowed everything. Then all was quiet for a while, till the solemn hush was troubled, and the most cruel thunderstorm rent the air that it has ever been my lot to witness. This lasted for three mortal hours. Four times the vivid lightning was followed *immediately* by a thunderclap which seemed to show us that there was only a moment's breathing-space between us and eternity. It was as though the clouds could not tear themselves away, but kept wandering round the hills of Sandakan letting off their apparently pent-up fury over the harbour where we were. Although the thunder presently ceased, still the rain kept falling in water-spouts, and as our cabin opened on the decks we were obliged to remain with the doors closed, so that it was miserably hot inside.

At length the cloudy morning broke, and relief came to our wearied souls when we were nearly stifled. We scrambled ashore out of that dripping steamer, and having slimed like snails up the clayey paths to our former abode, we found that in spite of the bungalow having been built on the side of a well-drained sandy hill, the rainfall during the night had been so excessive that all the bottom floors were under water.

CHAPTER XXIII

NATIVES OF NORTH BORNEO

In Borneo the Dyaks are a race of shortish men, but not nearly so short or so small as the Malays. I was told that they were exceedingly plucky. There were some Dyaks in the 'North Bornean Police' (this is merely a name, as they are really soldiers), although the company who owns North Borneo has imported a quantity of Sikhs from India, who are remarkably fine looking men, on purpose for this police work. Still they have some Dyaks amongst their forces. These men could not stand the English way of making war with the rifle. They looked at the thing from this point of view: there is no fun in just standing behind a rifle while you let it off, no danger, and very little agony to be seen; it does not require any heart-rending excitement to shoot an enemy down from a distance—in fact, the use of a rifle is altogether too slow a way of doing the job. These Dyak policemen, when they have fired one shot at their adversaries, like to throw away their guns and dash in with a knife, yelling like madmen. Then when they see blood streaming in every direction they *are* pleased; for this is the form of butchery they love. It is no wonder that the company should import Sikhs for their work, who in dealing with the natives use rifles which they let off *only* when they are ordered to. The Dyak's way of doing the job, although it must require a certain amount of pluck, will not do in modern warfare.

The Sulus are another native race. They are tall men—in fact, the only tall men that I saw in Borneo—and in addition to being tall, they are *sinewy*, thin and strong. To say that Sulus never grow fat would be going too far, but I have never seen one out of the scores who come in boats from their native island—Sulu Island—who had an ounce of superfluous flesh on his body. They are certainly very well built, almost all of them having a slight tendency to bandy legs; this I should think they had acquired from generation after generation sitting the whole of their lives in boats, and paddling in a cramped up position. Their figures together with their native dress make them appear strangely spindly objects. Neither the Sulus nor any of the natives in North Borneo seem to have any hair on their faces, except a very slight attempt at a moustache. Their complexion is naturally very light for an Eastern race; many of them are about the same colour as a very much sun-burnt Englishman. Take a dark-haired Englishman who has been for a trip up the Thames in a boat during a sunny August, and the skin of his face will be just as brown as that of one of these natives.

The Sulus all wear the native costume. First come the feet, which are bare; then the legs, on which there is a kind of linen trowsers, so tight that it is said a Sulu having once put them on finds it impossible ever to get out of them again. This is of course a libel; however, they are perfectly glove-like, as they fit close into the legs, till you get up to what we used to call as children their 'sit upon,' when they get so appallingly loose that you can put three ordinary men into them. These garments leave plenty of room, more room inside than is necessary. But it is difficult to say to what lengths fashion will lead, and this is the Sulu fashion.

They have what we call in Ceylon a cumberbund of gaudy silk round their waist, holding in the many loose folds of their pantaloons. Above that comes a cotton tight-fitting jacket, which is infinitely too short in the waist and too tight about the arms. This collarless jacket is buttoned across the chest with six braided buttons, like some pyjama jackets at home, with a slit up each side above the hips. They all wear hats made out of the same leaves as the house roofs, which end in a point about one foot above the brim.

We had a native boat built under our own supervision in Sandakan. It was ordered by Van a month before we came to Borneo, and had been scooped out with the greatest care by a native. Since our arrival this native had been suffering from a sickness in the leg, to which we had devoted a mother's tenderness. It was at length, through Van's administrations with a bottle of medicine, and my continual presence fidgeting round the bed, getting much better. Therefore we supposed that in return for our kindliness he had taken the greatest trouble in building the boat. It was forty feet long, built of a single log of wood scooped out, with three rims of boards up above and glued together at the seams with dammar or resin. There was an awning of palm leaves constructed over its centre, so that we might find some shade aboard. We then engaged fifteen natives to paddle the ship, and sent her off with our heavy baggage to the Segaliud River, whither we decided to follow a few days later. We intended to go altogether about forty-five miles from Sandakan, twenty odd miles of which were across the salt waters of the bay, and twenty miles up the mouth of the little Segaliud River. We therefore connected this native boat to a steam launch which belonged to one of the two estates up the river, and started her off on May 10. We left Sandakan ourselves on the 14th in a steam launch called the 'Despatch,' which we had chartered for the purpose.

On our way up the river's mouth we passed many a mangrove-covered island. The long branches of the mangrove trees were apparently resting upon those dreamily tinted waters, with strings of green seeds hanging down two feet at least, till here and there they touched the still reflecting sea. Away over the calm sunny waters the light blue distance seemed to rest on uncertain nothingness, while a slight mirage filled up the eastern horizon behind. We noticed the mangrove trees growing innumerable roots from every branch that extended over the watery soil, so that there was great difficulty in seeing accurately amid the mass of rooted branches where one tree ended and another began.

As we found ourselves further up the river there were other sorts of mangroves, very like our English birch trees, but with rather larger leaves and not quite such white stems. Then presently we came to 'nepah palms,' the leaves of which stretched sometimes *thirty* feet out of the now encroaching tide.

The nepah leaves are without stem or trunk at all above the soil; they rear themselves aloft, like enormous ferns waving in the gentle breeze in a soft and weary way beneath the blazing tropical sunlight. Soon we reached higher land, which seemed overpowered with towering jungle trees, till at last we came to a standstill.

On this ship we took a cock with us, that had been given to Van as a parting peace-offering by a devoted old native in Sandakan. This fowl ate all day—indeed, it seemed foolish to give it rice because of its magnificent appetite. It also crowed continually in the most provoking tone of voice. After a while we began to hate it with a Satanic hatred. Then we were wrecked —but of this I will tell you more anon—and we fain hoped in our secret souls that this bird would be left behind. But just as we were putting off in our boat from the wreck he gave one heartrending crow; we therefore felt obliged to put back and collect him from the high bows of the ship. The first night ashore that cock remained pretty silent; this, however, did not last long, as the following morning he was, goodness knows why, so very proud of himself that he made the surrounding forest ring with his inharmonious voice. Then we took counsel together and determined to slay him, as it was impossible to go on being exasperated and almost driven crazy by this brute. So he was killed, and very lean he turned out to be in spite of his voracious appetite.

We had intended going about a mile further up the river than we eventually did, but the way was not so open as it should have been. The tide was falling fast, and the native captain did not know the water, so that we presently ran right on to a log of wood. The bows of the steamer were hoisted out of the water, and her stern was almost beneath it. As we were going at full speed, and suddenly came to a dead standstill, the shock was very violent. We should have remained there about six hours, until the tide, which was falling, had risen again; but fortunately the boat which we had sent on before, was waiting for us at a native house about a mile further up the river. When we had whistled furiously at intervals of five minutes for about half an hour, she came round a corner and rescued us. We travelled on merrily to a campong, where we stopped the night, and the following morning, having bundled ourselves, our tents, our cooking apparatus, and our guns into the boat, proceeded about four miles up the stream till we came to a cleared landing stage. Here we disembarked, and having loaded our boatmen with all the things, we walked three miles from the river to a tobacco estate, where we put up for the night. This, like all other tobacco estates in Borneo, was an almost flat tract of about three hundred acres of cut down forest.

I am told that the tobacco grown in this country has an advantage over that of Sumatra, because of its burning a much whiter ash, and nothing could be more spotlessly white than the ash of certain Bornean cigars which we smoked. I was, however, informed that they only grow tobacco suitable for the outside roller of cigars in Sumatra, so that this wrapper, although very well grown, may be completely spoiled by having inferior tobacco placed within its folds. It is also very doubtful whether tobacco becomes improved by the voyage to Amsterdam before being converted into cigars.

CHAPTER XXIV

ELEPHANTS

We only stayed one day on this estate; the next morning we started off with fourteen of our boat's crew carrying our tent and provisions and enough rice for four days' absence in the jungle. We wanted to discover the whereabouts of some elephants which we had heard were to be found in these parts. Elephants are only to be found in the northern provinces of this island, between the Labuk River on the north and St. Lucia Bay on the south. Why elephants should exist on this north-eastern part of the island and not all over Borneo is a matter of speculation, but the most satisfactory answer that can be found is, that they are only the offspring of certain elephants brought over here years ago from the island of Sulu, when they were turned out and increased in numbers enormously till their present state. Sulu is a few hundred miles to the east of North Borneo.

Besides the fourteen men, we had told about six natives from the campong to come up, as they said they knew all about the jungle. In addition to this our party consisted of our four servants and ourselves.

First we had to see all the things packed, and that

VAN'S NATIVE SERVANTS FROM JAVA.

all the men had a good meal of rice before starting, and finally we did not get off till nine o'clock in the morning.

We walked about two miles over the clearing, and then nearly six miles into the jungle, where we pitched our tent in what seemed to be the dampest and most dripping spot on the face of the earth; not that it was really damper or more dripping than other portions of this interminable forest, but it *was* moist. From here we started off walking in different directions looking for fresh elephant tracks, as we had seen nothing but 'spoor' three or four days old crossing our trail. I believe an elephant travels an enormous distance every day amid the innumerable multitudes of square miles of jungle which surround it on every side.

We spent two days in this way, going out separately and searching about for fresh tracks, but finding none. If there had been any we should have been sure to come across them, as although an elephant leaves hardly any impression on the leaves of the higher ground with his flat feet, still he is bound to cross the muddy parts of the forest, where we saw plenty of old tracks.

Our tent was pitched on the side of what was called a 'cutting.' These 'cuttings' are made by the surveyors, partly in order that the owners of the new tobacco estates may form an opinion as to the lie of the land, and sometimes for purposes of Government survey. They are formed by cutting down the jungle in a perfectly straight line, generally east by west, or north by south.

On the second day I lost my way—as who that is

fresh to this jungular travel would not? I was walking with two men: one was my gun-bearer, and the other a silent man from the campong, but a fellow in whom I could place the greatest confidence. We had nothing to guide us but my compass. At about two o'clock the sun became clouded, and it began to rain in the usual tropical manner, so that my leader paused, as not being able to see the sun he did not know in which direction to go; then I had to direct him to the best of my possible knowledge with the compass. It seemed, however, that I was a point or two wrong, as eventually after wandering about helplessly for a couple of hours, we got out into a boundary cutting which we had not either of us seen before. I was for turning to the right, which would lead us in an easterly direction, and the silent man was doubtful which way to go. Eventually, after picking up two sticks and looking very wisely at their ends, he examined the ground most carefully and decided to go to our left in a westerly direction. Thinking that he ought to know more about it than I did, I followed meekly. It was now five o'clock, and we knew that by twenty minutes past six it would be pitch dark, so we pushed forward as hastily as possible, till at length we came to a turning at right angles to the cutting along which we were walking. Knowing that our tent was on one of these cuttings going north by south, we hastened down it, hoping that it would lead us campwards. As there were three or four cuttings going in the same direction, it was very doubtful whether we had struck the right one. Fortunately, just as darkness was coming over us, we heard a rifle being fired by Van, who was giving us up as lost.

We reached camp in a very exhausted condition. Then I asked why my guide, when he was doubtful of our whereabouts, had picked up bits of wood and looked so carefully at their ends? and learned the following piece of information: when you get thirsty, as there is no drinkable water you have to apply to your guide, who has probably lived in the vicinity of these forests all his life; he cuts down the thick stem of a particular jungle creeper and carries it to you horizontally, then by turning it up vertically over your mouth, a stream of water issues forth which is very clean and wholesome, as it has percolated through the soil, and been gathered up by the roots of the creepers.

Van, we knew, had gone out to our north-east that morning, and when my guide found recently-cut bits of wood from this creeper lying on the ground amongst the débris, he was sure that they were left by Van's men, which gave him a clue to our whereabouts.

How gorgeous our camp fare seemed after being so many hours in the dripping jungle; and how luxurious our bed as we crawled beneath the mosquito curtains! Stretching our wearied limbs, we soon floated away into dreamland, and were at rest.

It is impossible to stop up reading in camp after dinner, not only because of your utter prostration, as this tropical exercise takes all the energy out of you, but the flies and moths are so numerous after candle time, that it seems much the best thing to get beneath the mosquito netting, and, if possible, shut out the fever-stricken fog which nightly creeps round on all sides.

Van asked me before turning in that evening what

sort of jungle it was that I had been roaming through? I said it was just the same as any other jungle—a mass of awfully big ants, and here and there a crowd of smaller ones intermingled with leeches. It was the most tangled walking that I had ever known in my life, hot, wet, and smelling of decaying vegetation.

As we could find no fresh elephant tracks, we decided that we had better get out of this crowd of singing insects and make up the Segaliud River to another locality where we had also heard that elephants had been seen. As soon as it got light, therefore, on the following morning, we packed all our things, leaving nothing standing except the tent, beneath which the men lit two fires in the hopes of drying it, while we walked on towards the estate.

When we had accomplished about four miles of our homeward journey, we saw some quite fresh rhinoceros tracks in the muddy sides of one of the many almost stagnant watercourses that we had continually to cross. We at once started after this rhinoceros, as it is possible with the most dogged care to follow the trails of this animal. When we had slowly meandered along for about a mile—which must have taken us three-quarters of an hour—we came to what is called a 'salt lick,' which is where these beasts love to go and refresh their souls with a taste of salt. Here the rhinoceros had evidently been enjoying himself that morning, as the dirty pools were thick with mud, and the marks were apparent where he had got out and left the water. He had probably not gone more than half an hour, as the pools of water in his footmarks were still agitated and clouded with dirt.

Then we proceeded almost noiselessly, when *suddenly* not more than forty yards before us we heard the bushes and undergrowth moving—we stood in breathless silence—presently the jungle trees were parted whence the sound came, and a huge elephant, instead of the rhinoceros we were following, came out and then disappeared in the bush again, feeding right across in front of us, as this was about ten o'clock in the morning. There were apparently no others accompanying him, as we could hear no other sound but the millions of crickets singing in the sunlight from the tree tops. We therefore crept forward till only about twenty-five yards intervened between us and the spot where the elephant *ought* to be; the top of his head presently emerged from behind the screen of trees.

By this time we both had our eight-bores ready to fire, and I was only waiting to get a good sight before I let off mine: however, Van got the first chance, and, although it was fairly my turn to shoot, he could not resist the temptation, and with one shot dropped him dead with a bullet through the brain. Immediately after firing there was a noise through the jungle as of something heavily retiring, which must have been the rhinoceros, as on pressing forward to the stream-bed where our dead elephant had crossed, there were only the quite fresh tracks of a *single* elephant, and the equally fresh tracks exactly in the same place, only going in a different direction, of a single rhinoceros. Of course when a rhinoceros has been disturbed so closely, it is ridiculous trying to catch him up, so we returned to our elephant.

I believe this was the only elephant that had been

killed *by hunting* in the island of Borneo, although a Mr. Allard had shot one which he came on suddenly when rowing up the Keenabatangan River. I do not include those elephants which have been killed by natives, as we calculated that the more warlike tribes of North Borneo must have slain at least two since the day when Noah got out of the ark.

The elephant we had shot was a beautiful old tusker; he only possessed a few black hairs at the top of his head, about the size of the hairs of a clothes brush, and a few more at the end of his tail, as thick as the thickest bell wire. His body, which was hairless, was brown, and his height at the shoulder was seven feet nine inches; we took this by measuring one of his fore feet round the outside, and doubling the circumference. His tusks were three feet three inches and a quarter in length, and he was altogether, as the nigger said when the railway engine ran over his wife, 'the bulliest old efferlant that ever I seen.'

Van said, 'The worst of these elephants is that they leave no tracks behind them when on the higher ground of the jungle, as they have such a soft way of treading and such wonderfully flat feet; unlike the rhinoceros and the tapir, which are possessed of only three sharp toes on each fore foot, they have five toes, which only just come down to the ground.'

We promptly sent the men home the four miles which intervened between us and the estate, whilst we waited three hours and a half for their return. A hungry time that was, but not altogether desolate, as we had the elephant's carcase to keep us company; also enormous flies, almost as big as cockroaches, which immediately settled on his body, consoled us in part. We had only brought a breakfast of rice with us, which by seven o'clock in the morning had been consumed, so that we had to wait by that defunct corpse till three o'clock in the afternoon, wet through and miserably empty.

It had rained for half an hour, descending during that interval in lumps—as it rains in bigger things than drops in Borneo. It comes down perfectly straight; you can therefore find no shelter beneath a tree, and it is preferable standing out in the open and letting the rain descend in its natural course, to receiving it in wine-glass loads from the boughs above.

They came back eventually with Mr. Kalfsterman, our host, bringing basket-loads of food. A number of Chinese coolies came to cut up and carry home the feet, skin, tail, ears, and tusks of the elephant. They also took with them large pieces of flesh for comestible purposes. At length we were able to slide over those now muddy tracks and reach the bungalow and rest.

On this trip we had one more day's hunting, when we shot an enormous bull bison. But on May 25 we left our hospitable host, because we were compelled to leave, not that we wanted to, as in such a doubtful country it is not every day that one meets a Mr. Kalfsterman by whom one is treated as a little lord in disguise.

After rowing down six miles of the river we came to the 'Punch,' a steam launch which was to take us back the forty odd miles to Sandakan Harbour.

CHAPTER XXV

LABUAN

I STAYED some days more in Sandakan, and then said good-bye to the place for ever, as Van had business which called him away, and without tents or any knowledge of the language I could not go out shooting alone.

After circumnavigating North Borneo again on our way back to Singapore, we at length arrived at Labuan. This island is only six miles at the nearest point from the coast of Borneo; but in looking out from the harbour at Victoria across the intervening sea, owing to the flatness of the land you would think that it was a considerable distance, and that the far off hazy mountains must be miles and miles away. It is true that they are some leagues away, but not nearly so far as they appear. In this feature they differ so strongly from the Ceylon mountains, which in the dry season can be seen standing out distinct and clear almost all the day, whereas the Bornean hills are always crowned with cloud, except sometimes in the very early morning.

Labuan certainly is a redeemed spot in this ocean filled with jungle-covered lands. It has now been under British rule for forty odd years, and although it seems falling out of repair, still it looks like an old English place.

When you get under the shadow of the wide-spreading trees, and see the lovely green turf around, the native houses standing back from the now grass-grown roadway, the brick-made gate-posts which remain without any gates to support them, you begin to understand that this island was intended to show the Eastern Pacific England's greatness, but has never realised its dream. Labuan is a heavenly shady place, an island where the ground has all been cultivated for years, an island which *seems* as though it had been the ideal which the British intended to make it, but is so no longer.

If you go up the hill to the empty Government House about two miles away from the town, and see what a beautiful cattle-fed park surrounds it with all sorts of wealthy shade-giving trees, if you gaze at the pretty little toy palace with its tennis lawn and shady plantations, it makes you almost shed a tear to see what glories were provided by the British Government for an English governor who exists no longer. The governor of British North Borneo now acts as governor of Labuan, and his residence of course is at Sandakan; for although North Borneo is not directly under British rule, but merely beneath the British protectorate, Labuan has always been one of our colonies. This little island, with not more than two dozen letter-writing people on it, has its own stamps, for it is a separate British colony.

There is a company which has lately been formed for working a coal mine on this far-off little island, a coal mine which was worked years ago, and then as no ships came down to these waters it was abandoned; but now as North Borneo is gradually becoming better known a new company has been started, a fresh opening has been formed to the mine, and already, we were told by our engineer, it turns out coal that is only fifteen per cent. inferior to the coal of Cardiff.

Beneath the trees of which I spoke and which are called by the natives 'Angseuna' trees, I met a quantity

ANGSEUNA TREES, LABUAN

of ladies who were chiefly remarkable for certain silver buttons which they wore down their dark-blue clothes. Many of them were quiet-looking girls, who had been into Victoria to sell the produce of the land. I was told that they were 'Kadayans,' a tribe, or part of a tribe, who originally lived in Brunei, but through oppression and slavery forced on them by the Sultan came over to Labuan to settle. They are strictly an agricultural race, very quiet and well behaved, and there must be some two thousand of them now settled in Labuan. There was only one objection to the Kadayans which seemed serious—namely, that I could not speak to them, as I was not familiar with their tongue, and could not get them to stand still to be photographed.

The people in the village of Victoria were chiefly Chinese, but there were two groups of native houses across the other side of the bay, about half a mile distant, which were altogether inhabited by Malays. These houses were built on piles driven into the sea, about ten yards away from the land. The natives approached their dwellings in quite ridiculously small 'dug outs,' so low in the water that they continually shipped little seas, and consequently had to be bailed out every three strokes.

The folks in these villages supply the outer world with bananas and 'kadjangs.' These latter articles are the young leaves of the palm called 'nepah,' which being dried in the sun become yellow and tough enough to paper the walls of all the native houses. Perhaps to 'paper the walls' is the wrong way of expressing it; the walls are built of wooden scaffolding, covered with one layer of palm leaves; these with the heavily thatched roofs, made from the older leaves of the same palm, keep the houses wonderfully cool.

We could not at first get a lodging here, as the six British residents had no room they could offer us, and we had almost returned shipwards again in despair, intending to go on to Singapore, when someone with the utmost presence of mind said, 'Why should you not try the Government *rest house*?'

We never knew that there was such a place; even our informant seemed doubtful about its existence. We then made inquiries as to its locality, and one man thought that there *was* a rest house, while another was not sure whether it was two miles from the city or four.

We were not to be done, and set out resolutely to search the island, which occupies about thirty square miles. We thought that it was only owing to our unprecedented tracking powers that at length coming to a cocoa-nut planted field, over which the water from a brook coursed down in un-bebanked freedom; seeing a small palm-leaved house across the swampy floor, we concluded that this was the Government rest house, which it proved to be.

The most abandoned dirty-looking Chinaman was the guardian of this heavenly spot. It was, as I said before, a *Government rest house*, which accounted for a good deal—accounted for there only being one mosquito netting, instead of two, as written in the bill of fare, and for all sorts of little things which with the assistance of our boys we were able to correct.

We eventually got settled in this little three-roomed bungalow. It was situated on a hill about two miles away from the town and harbour. We had first to order everything in the way of food that we wanted, and wait patiently while this presiding Chinaman, who was decidedly slow, carried the articles the two miles uphill from the town, which *is* trying if you happen to be hungry.

One day, having nothing better to do, we hired a canoe, with five Malay men to paddle it, and went out to a little wooded island across the sea, called Poolau

Papan, taking our guns with us, as we thought we might get some pigeons there. Our boat was propelled with five oblong-bladed paddles, which the Malays worked sitting flat on the boards at the bottom, but otherwise exactly as the Canadians paddle their birch-barks.

When we first started we concluded that this canoe had just been taken from a bath beneath the sea, because it was extremely wet. Too soon, however, we found out that in this we had been mistaken. The tropical sun presently rose in an all-consuming orb, when the boat became almost unwholesome from the sour smell of bad fish, emanating from its steaming interior. Fortunately the men paddled hard, so that we soon got across that breathless sea, or we might have sickened from the smell of decaying fish.

I never saw a more tropical condition of treey luxuriance than that island presented, with the boughs of many of the trees stretching out over the sea at high water. However, we could not penetrate the mass of foliage, and our shooting was a failure. Some of the trees were full of birds, especially one which was bearing fruit; the upper branches seemed crowded with winged fowl of every sort.

There were some fishing natives upon this island who had evidently lived there while they cut up enough drift wood to make fires for all the village of Victoria during a fearful and stormy winter season, which period they were now waiting for. To judge by the amount of wood which they had stacked away, I should say that they had been waiting expectant for at least ten years. Some of these natives were now quite old and infirm, and my friend said ' that he judged that if they waited till that winter season came on, they would be older and infirmer by long chalks than they were then.'

It seemed a peaceful enough life to live beneath the shadow of a great forest, chopping firewood and fishing away their existence, a life which I yearned to waste with these natives if it had not been for the smell of dead fish which surrounded them. Out here, of course, there is no one who is fool enough to buy their wood, and therefore they have to catch fish to live on.

There are a multitude of fish everywhere about North Borneo, as, unlike the Mediterranean, there is a tide here, and the sea is not too salt. I believe the natives are not allowed to sell fish in Labuan—in fact, it is the most difficult thing in the world to obtain fish for food there, as I understand a certain Chinaman buys from Government the monopoly of selling fish, and in a most un-Christian way puts such an exorbitant price on it that the ordinary mortal cannot afford to buy any. These natives with the utmost care catch infinitely more fish than they need; the surplus rot away in the sun, so that they smell appallingly, and my friend said, 'The smell of bad fish was so apparent that he could almost divide it with his hand.' He declared that it was visible. A visible smell does not even read pleasantly.

We watched these men boiling rice, or steaming rice perhaps I ought to say, as they boiled the water in a brass pot, over the mouth of which they put a bit of bamboo containing the rice, and thus steamed it till it was cooked.

Then we returned to Victoria, bearing with us the result of our morning's outing—viz., one pigeon.

CHAPTER XXVI

BRUNEI

THE next morning we started off in a very weather-beaten and rickety old steam launch which happened to be going down to Brunei. A Chinaman was to provide us with a certain amount of food for our journey, and during our stay there, which we thought would occupy us about four days. We left it to this Chinese gentleman to put up exactly what he thought would be right for our requirements. These are the items as he put them aboard the boat, copied from the bill :—

> Two small tins of potted tongue.
> Two of butter.
> Two of Messrs. Moir & Co.'s strawberry jam.
> One (minute) tin of biscuits.
> One bottle of whisky.
> Two dozen bottles of soda water.
> *Eight dozen* bottles of beer.
> One corkscrew (stolen from us by the crew).
> Three glasses (one stolen).

This was all!

The drink part of the menu seems rather overbalanced, but we have no means of reckoning what a Chinaman will expect you to do.

Brunei is an independent state between North Borneo and Sarawak. It is governed by the weakest and most easy-natured *looking* old Sultan, who, I am told, will not hold his sway much longer, as Sarawak and North Borneo both have an eye on the country, and are both longing to annex it. There seemed every probability of this taking place before even this aged gentleman was hidden beneath the tomb.

The Sultan of Brunei is what a young Englishman who was my companion, and whom we will name 'Slope,' called 'an indifferent and carnal old cuss.' He lives in his own palace, in his own chief town, on his own river, and has twenty wives of his own.

I believe that the Sultan of Brunei formerly owned the greater portion of North Borneo, but now, how are the mighty fallen! already the principal chiefs of certain tribes have sent to Rajah Brooke, begging him to rule over them instead of this grasping, ill-regulated old Sultan, as they cannot afford to pay the taxes heaped on them by him.

The town of Brunei is situated many miles up the tidal waters of a river called the Brunei River, in the territory of Brunei. There is one advantage about this country—viz., that the word Brunei carries you a long way.

This native town was built entirely of wood and palm leaves, on piles driven into the ground beneath the water's surface in the middle of this tidal stream. The Brunei River happens to be broad where the town is situated, and I should say there was considerable depth in its centre, where the stream flows, as there was a channel or broad street up the middle where no houses were built. We only saw two or three dwellings on the banks; all the rest were constructed on piles in the river. The picture is from a photograph, and shows the more thickly-peopled side of the channel. You may guess what sort of appearance the city has, when I tell you that there are about eighteen thousand inhabitants, all living in these palm-leaved houses, raised about two feet above high-water mark. With the exception of a few Chinese traders, the people live a simple, lazy, am-

TOWN OF BRUNEI ON PILES

bitionless existence. They are all Mahommedans, and consequently teetotallers.

But I am hurrying on too fast. We came down to Brunei, a distance of forty miles from Labuan, in a steam launch, which certainly was of the dirtiest and most inferior description. It was manned by a Malay crew, whose honesty and capability of restraining themselves were of the lowest type. However, they carried us down safely and only captured four of our bottles of beer, a couple of pineapples, and a corkscrew, when our boy was not looking. Missing beer when you know that there is plenty of it is not like beer deferred, for drink deferred maketh the heart *very* sick.

Talking of pineapples reminds one that they were remarkably cheap at Brunei. We gave our servant twenty cents (about eightpence) to buy a pineapple, and when we went down to the cabin there were eighteen ripe pineapples on the bench. Then Slope said quite angrily to the boy, ' Why did you buy such a lot ? Do you want to feed a whole girls' school ; can't you see that we have not got one aboard ? ' The boy said that he had only bought twenty cents' worth, the same as master told him.

No sooner had we arrived at Brunei than a quantity of natives came on board the launch. One old gentleman first shook hands with us all round and then began talking most confidentially to Slope in an undertone, and, as it appeared afterwards, in an unknown tongue. My friend said at once, looking across at me, ' Let us dissemble: perhaps he is a spy.' Then he stepped aside with the old man, who for about five minutes appeared to be whispering things unheard-of in his ear. Presently Slope said quite audibly, ' Ah, ha, what is this ? ' and he began to roam the decks with unspeakable agony depicted in every pore of his skin. Then I said to him, ' Compose yourself, and when you can cease this roving spirit take me into your confidence ; unbosom yourself to me, and I will be a sharer in your desolation.' He took me aside and remarked in a confidential undertone : ' Well, look here, it is just like this, old man—I can't understand a syllable that this aged warrior keeps pouring into my ears; what shall I do? for I am afraid that he is talking something about beer.'

At this moment the native captain came up and said quite distinctly, 'You must take care, there is much steal man aboard.' Upon which Slope exclaimed, 'My God, and is it thus I am to die? I have brought no weapons with me, and this man of iron

A HOUSE IN BRUNEI

has followed me even here.' However, after a while we managed to disband the offensive old man, and we noticed in bidding him our final adieux that when he was pretending to pay attention to our remarks he was, like many a small boy at home, much troubled with his nose.

We then elected to go and call on the Sultan of Brunei, as we thought that he would be just the man to see us out of any difficulty we might have got into with this aged native. We started off in a very small Brunei boat, which resembled a walnut shell, to visit his Imperial Highness.

I got in first because I had a great idea of getting myself settled, as a kind of ballast, before Slope, who was a heavy young man, should descend into this teaspoon of a boat. Then Slope got aboard, and having shipped a quantity of water we found ourselves under way.

Arrived before his kingly portals, we clambered up a ladder and found ourselves in the Throne Room or Council Chamber. It was an iron-roofed room, rendered as uncomfortable as possible by having four wooden kitchen chairs round a central dirty wooden table. There were no gilded guards, no attendants, nor anything to indicate royalty, except a rather dilapidated and very comfortless-looking gilt chair raised on a piece of wood called a dais at one end of the room, which, by the way, the old man did *not* sit on.

Here we waited for awhile, considering who should occupy the position of spokesman.

By and bye the old monarch, whose name in short is Sultan Hashim Jalilud Alam Akamadin—the name in the Directory occupies three lines, but there is not room for the whole of it in this page—approached smoking what we at first thought was a churchwarden pipe, but which proved afterwards to be a cigarette a foot long covered with a white palm leaf. He had no one in attendance, and we watched him sauntering across a sort of open yard—if a house on piles can be said to have a yard—where a lot of naked children and fowls were playing, till he came to anchor in the iron-roofed room where we were waiting.

The introduction was then struggled through. We briefly told him in our best Malay that we had come down to see his city, the renown of which had gathered us in from afar, in order to call and pay our most humble respects to one who merited much more than we could do for him (this was too true, as we neither had done, nor intended to do, anything for this sovereign); we hoped that handfuls of blessings might ever rest on his undiminished head, etc.

I do not think that he understood our best Malay words—in fact, we got them so mixed up that we could not make head or tail of them ourselves; we certainly did not understand him, except when he presently wanted to know for how much we would sell the launch. As it was not ours we had to put an exorbitant price on it. Then he evidently considered whether it would be safe to seize it or no, and eventually decided that as Rajah Brooke was then in his, the Sultan's, territory, this would not be a politic thing to do. So having given us some of the groundiest coffee it has ever been my fortune to encounter, and some cigarettes like his own, which were capital smoking, he sat and looked at us till we did not think that we were getting any 'forarder.' Then we concluded to go, and went. His people eyed us curiously.

As we were paddled away in the little walnut shell, the rush blinds of the houses in the immediate vicinity were cautiously drawn aside, and we were treated to the furtive glances of what we thought were about eighteen of his wives. These ladies are not particularly dark, and with their long black hair done up in a knot on the top of the head, seemed decidedly pretty. They laughed pleasantly at us, displaying the usually fine teeth of tropical women, and were evidently but little accustomed to white faces.

After a silence of a few minutes I asked Slope what he thought of the Sultan. 'I should say,' returned he rather pompously, 'that the Sultan Hashim Jalilud Alam Akamadin was the personification of intense greatness, illumined—as they say in a most interesting weekly pamphlet called "Fun" which I have forwarded me from home—by limitless mental and physical versatility; that these were his leading characteristics. Did you see how his eyes gleamed with a sudden fire when I told him that the launch could only be bought for many thousands of dollars, and that even then I must ask the consent of the owners before parting with her? Ah, yes, I think he is indeed a great man, and I felt, as we entered his lordly palace like one of the knights of old going to call on the Dey of Tunis; but his attendants certainly looked askance at us.'

Soon after this the launch left again for Labuan, so that we found ourselves deserted in this water city.

CHAPTER XXVII

BRUNEI —(*continued*)

WE came armed with a letter to one Inche Mahommed, the British Consul in these parts. He was a Malacca follower of the Prophet, and had an infinitely better house than the Sultan. To his abode, therefore, we wended our way, as of course there was no hotel in this native place, and we thought that he would be certain to put us up.

The Moslem, however, was sick; yes, sick unto death. When, therefore, we heard that he could not entertain us on this account, we looked at one another in the most despondent way, and simply gulped and blinked, for this was sad.

However, when we had got away in our walnut shell again, and made a slight luncheon off pineapples and whisky, we felt better, and after cruising around this town on piles we eventually disembarked at the most superior house of a *most* superior Chinaman, who what you may call 'extended himself' as much as possible. He spoke a few words of our tongue, and very kindly cleared out a loft over a kerosene oil and sago store for our accommodation. This store was very dark all day, it smelt horribly of stale sago and rats, so that until you had climbed up a ladder in the thick smelling darkness it was not pleasant to feel your way through. Then you saw an enormous beamed wooden loft, where our friend the Chinaman put two beds, and having cleared everything out but the rats, compensated for all drawbacks by the excellence of his cooking.

Slope remarked, after despatching our fourth bottle of beer, and performing more than his duty towards the food which had been prepared for our benefit that evening, 'I had thought of going up the Kinabatangan River and mingling with those native heathens in the backwoods of North Borneo, but think this is even better than living with the prospect of getting envenomed arrows driven into your ribs. Eh, what do you think?'

We were always hungry at Brunei; it mattered not if we had had no exercise, but had simply paddled round in the boat, there seemed something about those nauseous smells, arising from the falling tide or the aroma of the inhabitants, which distinctly created an appetite.

There was a single policeman in this city, who had evidently been told off by the Sultan to regard us carefully, as we supposed that he suspected us of fraud.

Our meals were prepared in a place which we thought was the family joss-house, as there was a kind of altar up at one end of the room, covered with brass things of a sort, and the walls were crowded with long black shiny boards about one foot broad and six feet long, which hung down like pendulums from the ceiling with immense Chinese characters carved on them and painted in gold. In this ancestor-gravestone-boarded dining-room we partook of what the poor folks at

NATIVE WOMEN AT BRUNEI

home call our 'wittles,' together with four great dogs belonging to the Chinaman, which always came in to see just what we were eating, and remained discovering fleas on their persons through the whole of our meals.

The Chinamen live on a small island in the middle of this river-paved town, and the street outside our dining-room was full of little Chinese children, who with a quantity of Malay men examined our performance through the door and the window bars with the most eager interest. It was then that the single policeman came in useful, as he constantly patrolled up and down making offensive noises at the children, and trying his utmost to frighten them away. At times, however, this seemed to be forgotten, for when we had a fresh course of curry the policeman could not resist the temptation of staring at us along with the rest of the inhabitants of the little island.

At first we thought it a bore having every mouthful of food that we ate criticised in a whispered undertone by such an admiring audience. But it is wonderful how one can become acclimatised to the scorching gaze of the multitude in this worn-out world. Anyway, *they* seemed to enjoy it and think us extraordinary.

It seemed, looking out at these naked savages, as though we had suddenly got back to the early morning of history. We were now in a country where almost every adjunct of civilisation was unknown—a country where marmalade, beer, and potatoes had never been introduced—and, after all, our being eyed from the street was merely savage curiosity.

Most of the children go about perfectly naked, living almost entirely in their little canoes, or in the water. We encountered some mere infants in midstream nearly a quarter of a mile from shore, in dugout canoes which were not more than a yard long, and looked as shallow as an ordinary saucer. One day we saw a party of eight naked boys paddling along at a great pace in a boat which could not have been more than two inches out of the river; when suddenly it struck against the branches of a fallen tree and capsized, pitching them all into the water. The lads seemed to enjoy this catastrophe, and laughing, soon brought the boat to the surface again, when having bailed all the water out with their hands, they crawled in one at a time, either over the bows or over the stern, till they were once more eight little laughing savages in that scooped-out piece of wood. They all seem to swim like ducks from the first moment of their existence in this wicked wide world.

Both the boys and girls play a most conspicuous part amidst the ever-bathing population of Brunei. When we first arrived we were greeted with shouts from twelve of these urchins, who were in the water, simply swimming and calling out in joyous tones at the top of their voices without any other object but enjoying themselves.

The women here are provided on the tops of their heads with a cross between an umbrella and a little roof in the shape of a hat, which comes down so low that when you see a boat from behind, you can discern nothing but two moon-shaped things like an archery target in it. You may be quite sure that there are two women before these, and it is made apparent that there is life on board the boat by the ends of paddles which keep dipping into the water as it progresses. These hats are made, as everything else is made out here, of nepah palm leaves. They come up to a central point, and are curved in a convex shape outside.

On our first arrival in port a crowd of little dug-outs had come alongside the launch, their owners having for sale Brunei tobacco, swords, and blow-tubes.

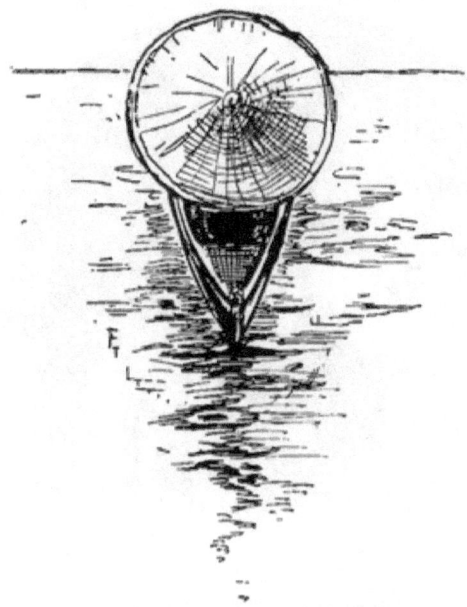

ALL THAT IS TO BE SEEN OF A BRUNEI BOAT RETIRING

These latter were rather a peculiar article of warfare. They were like a very minute gun-barrel, hollowed out of a piece of wood six feet long, up which are blown poisoned arrows. The gentleman who brought them had a quantity of these arrows, one of which he shot off for us to see. It was a little harmless-looking thing, and we could not conceive how he could hit any object, as there was no sight along the barrel.

In days gone by these people were a pretty powerful and warlike race, but they have *sadly* degenerated. Some of them cultivated little patches of ground with sago and fruits, while others fished; but they are easily contented, their wants are few, and none of them work hard. There appeared to be no army, and only the one policeman, whose office consisted in

THE BRUNEI STREET LAMP

moving on the audience who collected round our door as we fed. This minion of the law looked a weak-minded, good-natured old fellow, and the children seemed about as much afraid of him as we were.

There were, of course, no street lights in the town except one; this was a single smoky paraffin lamp, which looked unhappy and as if it laboured against its conscience in giving enough light for the many little boys to disband after we had done our meal, and for us to fall over the six Chinese dogs as we went to bed. I give a picture of it.

Up country the people seemed to be rather lawless, as a notice from the Sultan was posted up outside our door which appeared to be to the effect that a few miles up the river a tribe were busy *head hunting*; but, if this were the correct translation of the writing on the wall or not we shall never know, as the Chinaman who was our host was the only man in the whole town who spoke English, except poor Inche Mahommed, and he was sick unto death.

If this were true it will soon be put a stop to, as on one side the Rajah of Sarawak is now encroaching on this little empire, while on the other the British North Borneo Company are looking on hungrily. The day cannot be far distant, as I said before, when this apparently quiet little kingdom will be absorbed in the maw of civilisation, and from our point of view spoiled for ever.

The only thing we objected to in this primitive town were the smells upon our island home, as they were certainly most obnoxious. Fœtid odours came constantly up to our lofty bedroom window from a muddy blackness where the receding tide had left the banks all bare to the scorching sun. We could not keep them off except by going out in our boat and roaming about on the water, as they were infinitely worse in the sunlit day than in the night, when there was nothing but the moon to disturb the placid serenity of the river's bed.

We stayed at Brunei two or three days, cruising about in a family boat, as, like the rest of the inhabitants, we had to annex a boat to pace the street in. We wandered through the city taking photographs of nearly all we saw. I say of *nearly all*, as the females always ran away as soon as our eye was fixed on them. They hid behind palm-leaved screens, from which they either eyed us through holes punctured with their fingers in the cottage walls, or else looked out through cracks in the screens, as their curiosity to see our white skins was too obvious.

One morning when we came out to the market we found it crowded with boats filled with men and women who ought to have been selling one another their fish and egg produce, but out of curiosity they desisted altogether from their business whilst we were amongst them. We were looked at everywhere as quite strange beings, so that in wending our way amid the watery streets of the town we felt most incongruous mortals.

In certain parts of the river there were crowds of natives fishing with lines out of very long canoes. We paddled towards one of these collections and I counted as many as forty-six natives all fishing together. But in twenty minutes, while we waited by their side, after most diligently jerking their lines up and down, we gleed considerably—as we naturally took the part of the fish and not of their pursuers—to see that they collected nothing, and we saw no fish in their boats.

The Brunei River is a great stream with hills rising, I should say, about four hundred feet out of the apparently floating town.

One day we went to a sago factory which is carried on by Chinamen, and in which Chinese labour is wholly employed. The smell of sour sago which emanated from that spot was calculated to make you feel ill, if anything on this earth would. We therefore perspired up a hill about two hundred feet above the factory, to avoid the aroma; but even there we were attacked by it to such an extent that we found it necessary to descend by an exceedingly steep path—somewhat like the pigs in the Bible, only not into the sea. Down below we found the flavour if possible worse than it had been before. Thence we fled to a grass-grown graveyard beneath some shady trees. In this burying ground all the natives of Brunei have been interred since the beginning of creation. We thought to find peace for our souls amidst these vast tombs of sleeping Malays, but even here we were not safe, as the smell of sour sago penetrated beneath the thick foliage of those guardian jungle trees—trees which were waving over the tomb of many a warrior slain in the fray. Amid imprecations we left that solemn spot and rushed away down the wooden pier; we fled there with the ghastly smell of sour sago still haunting us. On, on we sped till at length, careless of all else, we threw ourselves into the boat, where, drifting away from the horrible spot, we at last found *rest*.

As this was a Sunday, Slope said to me after silently thinking for a long while, 'Do you suppose that the place which I shall visit in the hereafter will smell as badly as that sago factory? If so, I *swear* that from this day I will reform, because I could not—no—I *could not*, abide for a lifetime, without hopes of death, in such a spot.'

CHAPTER XXVIII

SINGAPORE

EVENTUALLY we left Brunei in a native boat paddled by eight of the inhabitants. It was the same boat we had used when we were the Chinaman's guests, large and open with a palm-leaved awning over its stern, where we sat. We feared, however, that it would not be large enough to face the sea in when we got out of Brunei Bay.

It is rather difficult to define the difference between the ocean proper and the land-encompassed sea in these Bornean tidal waters. All the ocean is so calm and placid, and you cannot discern the innumerable low-lying islands out at sea. However, we did not know if it would be calm enough to go all the way out to the island of Labuan, a distance of forty miles, in this little boat, or if we should only proceed to a place called Muara (pronounced Moira), fifteen miles along the Brunei inlet. There we could ask an Englishman called Mr. Peck whether we should continue our journey or no. This latter course we eventually decided to take.

Muara is a small peninsula dividing the sea-coast from the Brunei inlet. A few years ago this was purchased by the Rajah of Sarawak, as it contained some seams of coal. Out of the four mines I am told

A NATIVE FISHERMAN'S DWELLING NEAR MUARA

that the Rajah gets about a thousand tons per month, and now that he has put up regular English machinery over one of the pits he hopes shortly to be able to export double that quantity.

When we visited Brooketon—as the Rajah calls the spot where the coal mines are—there were sixty-three Chinese coolies working at the four mines, and between fifty and sixty Malays. Nearly all the coal-cutting was done by Chinese, who were paid about tenpence per truck, there being three trucks to the ton. The largest amount earned by a Chinaman in a month was about 16*l*. 6*s*. When we visited the place there were only two British residents there—viz., Mr. Peck and a Scotch engineer.

Muara only lay about three miles out of our direct course from Brunei to Labuan; at any rate, we were not wasting much time by calling there.

There was a small harbour down at the Muara landing, a miniature wooden pier, a great-little Chinese store and six or seven native houses placed on piles near the sea. About a mile and a half inland along a flat treeless plain there were a quantity of sandy hills; on the nearest of these was quite an important bungalow, surrounded by wide-spreading trees; this was the abode of Mr. Peck.

Unfortunately we had no letter of introduction to him, and were only two stray travellers who came to this shore in a native boat. Can you in England imagine anything more disagreeable than having two strange young men standing outside your door and waking you up from your afternoon nap by shouting 'boy' at the top of their voices, and when the boy appeared, not even knowing at whose portals they were standing? However, Mr. Peck came forward at this juncture, and most kindly introduced himself, so that we soon put our case before him, saying how we were travel torn, how we were two homeless voyagers who could not string three Malay words together without a fault in the genders, and how we had come to those shores with a boat-load of Brunei natives; how they apparently said, 'Do not venture further on this boiling ocean, as we have a quantity of fish at home which will go bad if we are drowned, and we shall never get back if we imperil our lives in this little craft.' We begged him to tell us what was best to be done under the circumstances.

He immediately telephoned down to a Malay man at the harbour to ask what sort of boat we had come in.

I must interrupt my story to tell you about this telephone, which was of the most novel construction, and had been laid down across the plain between the pier at Muara and the bungalow at Brooketon. Supposing on arriving at Muara you wished to send a message to Brooketon, it was impossible to do it without first sending a man across the intervening mile and a half to tell someone to listen at the other end of the telephone, as there was no bell or means of communication up at the bungalow. If, on the other hand, Mr. Peck wished to send a message down to the pier, he could ring such a clanging double bell that the coloured gentleman would rouse himself immediately and rush towards the telephone, if it were only to stop the overpowering noise. It was a most convenient telephone.

The result of this telephoning was that we were

most kindly asked to stay two or three days at Brooketon till a steam launch should be going to Labuan, as Mr. Peck did not think that our boat was large enough to cross the twenty-seven odd miles of sea. The boatmen were therefore told to carry our luggage up to the bungalow. They showed the greatest disinclination to carry our four little bags, and even when we had paid them more than they bargained for, eyed us curiously, for they were savage men.

Brooketon was a beautiful place. All this part of the country seemed to have been inhabited long years back, at a time which no one knows anything about, as there is no history of Brunei; nothing was apparent of the olden times, except the trees planted in clumps over the undulating ground. This was a land of mystery.

Upon the hills one was free from everything that was baneful to man. There were no leeches, scarcely any ants or flies; in fact, nothing which makes life disagreeable in other parts of Borneo. From the bungalow one looked out on a vast park-like expanse, where between the evergreen trees one saw masses of fern of every description filling up the little valleys in this grassy country.

We went out fishing twice with casting nets in the sea, and it was delightful beneath the shadow of numberless trees to paddle about on the sandy beach in the warm sunny waters, with Mr. Peck's five fox terriers following us. We enjoyed ourselves very much at Brooketon for three days, and then as the steam launch was going to Labuan, towing a native vessel full of coal, we had to say good-bye to Muara and proceed.

This steam launch was towing a native boat full of coal—of which I have given a photograph in the frontispiece of this book—and seemed to be suffering from bronchitis. It kept giving way to a short bark at intervals, as it crawled over the placid sea at about four knots an hour. However, eventually we arrived at Labuan, and on the following day a small *Chinese* steamer started for Singapore; on this we put our

BOYS BATHING BENEATH MY BUNK ABOARD THE BORNEO BOAT

luggage, and having said good-bye to some natives and Chinamen, we left these shores.

After being four days at sea, we came one evening in sight of the thousands of lights which flood the roads off the port of Singapore, and as we approached nearer and gradually nearer to that sea-reflected city, Slope said he felt like Satan nearing the confines of the earth. It did seem strange, after quitting the unsophisticated haunts of the Bornean native, to arrive once more in this busy hurrying world of gaslights and umbrellas.

Singapore has a magnificent hotel; the buildings are three hundred yards long, so that when the thermometer registers 88°, which is often the case, you become so exhausted in this damp climate, wandering along the heterogeneous corridors to get from the dining-room to your bedroom, that you are apt to dissolve altogether.

The grounds of the hotel are very pretty, if you admire a lawn dotted with green trees and scarlet hibiscus, with a peep of the ocean *filled* with ships, beyond. But of all the heartrending things that I ever came across, the mutton, the beef, the curry, and the soup which I endeavoured to consume at that magnificent hotel were the most galling.

Singapore is as greenly beautiful as Colombo, but it is filled with a broad-shouldered race of China*m*en, instead of the Singhalese and Mahommedans who people Ceylon. Why I lay a stress on the word *men* is because after living in Singapore for a week, I only saw about three Chinese women, and they were peeping out from behind wooden walls. There *must* have been Chinese women inside the blue-washed houses, but there were not a great number of children, and the female element is certainly a rarity, which seemed a pity considering the enormous number of men.

The huge population of Singapore, as a rule, know nothing of the English language, and travellers are led to suppose that in spite of its having been under British rule for seventy years, for some reason the Chinese have not been compelled to go to school, or learn anything of that glorious civiliser of the

Eastern world, the British tongue. Not only is our language unknown to the ordinary Chinese who form the greater part of the population, but other nationalities are equally unlearned and indifferent. If you take the Chinese jinrickshaw coolies, they are fine, manly looking fellows compared with the Malays; but there is not one jinrickshaw coolie out of the thousands you see flocking the streets who can speak two words of English. You would think, therefore, that you were anywhere but in a British colony, when you want to get to your friend's house which lies just round the corner.

These Malays are utterly different in appearance to the Singhalese. The Singhalese are a tall, bearded race of men: a crafty, subterfuging people, who look effeminately noble, and are utterly pluckless. Whereas these little Malays, although living as near the equator as the Singhalese, have a great deal of pluck 'of a sort' in them. They are as a rule very short, their features are much more 'squat,' and they seldom have any hair on their faces except a slight attempt at a thin moustache.

No one who has lived amongst them for a few weeks could mistake a Malay man for a Singhalese.

No one who has once seen the two nationalities *could* mistake a Singhalese for an ordinary negro, and yet I fear that many British ladies would not know one from the other. They speak of them all as 'those poor black fellows.' Take an English lady who has interested herself in foreign charities, and has perhaps in the course of her life given *pounds* to missionaries in various parts of the world, and I think that very often on seeing them she would not be able to distinguish between a bearded Singhalese and a stalwart Maori from New Zealand.

Have you ever watched a Chinaman undergoing the torture of being shaved? He first has the long threads of silk unplaited from his pigtail—these are hung up on a peg in the wall; then the combing out of his hair and the shaving begins. The Chinese barbers use a very sharp razor, but no soap; probably this is merely because they do not know where to put it, as no Chinaman whom I ever saw had a bristle of hair on his face. Nature has not endowed them copiously with hair except on the back of the head.

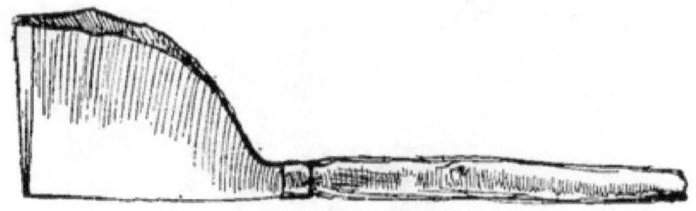

A CHINAMAN'S RAZOR

A man whom I was watching on one occasion was first shaved on the top of his head just above the forehead, where the bristles were about an inch long. Then the razor was carefully drawn down to where his whiskers ought to have been, after which the operator indulged in a few passes over the throttle. Now *the* work had really begun, and the barber sharpened up his razor on a morsel of leather just about the same size as his palm, which he held concealed in his left hand. Then he commenced shaving under the eyes, now above them, between the eyelashes and the eyebrows; here he found *a hair*, which he executed with one pass of the glittering instrument;

then he went on to the chin, where of course no hairs were to be found. At length, after half an hour and five minutes of this exquisite work, it was finished, and I began to breathe again, as the suspense of watching the operation had been so great that it had almost deprived me of my vital powers. The Chinaman had removed no less than fourteen hairs from his victim's face, and now that he had completed his

A CHINAMAN'S BOAT AT SINGAPORE

task his countenance assumed a look of triumph and delight.

When you get out of the town of Singapore the country becomes very pretty, as all the roads are planted along the sides with shade-giving tropical trees. Many of the bungalows are built of marble, and placed on small hills covered with Liberian coffee and mangosteen bushes, while enormous breadfruit trees hide them from the busy passing world outside.

The sight presented to an Englishman who for the

first time looks down a road on the outskirts of a town is very curious. The numbers of bullock bandies, jinrikshaws, and the native life with the indistinct distance of bluish dampness, combine in making a picture which it is difficult to forget.

CHAPTER XXIX

WE SET OUT ON OUR RETURN

It was June 25 when we left Singapore on our return journey. The air was moist and hot, and the regular tropical smell pervaded all things. The sky was clouded over, and everything that you touched was damp. In twenty days we should have left behind us this centre of perspiration and enervation, but first we had to pass through the Red Sea in July, which was a matter of dismal contemplation, at the thought of which, as they say in the hymn, 'Sank heart and voice oppressed.'

When I got on board my Messageries Maritimes steamer, the vessel was crowded with French people who were all talking at once. French people can talk. So do English folk—at least, in a girls' school. Presently, when the bell rang for visitors to leave the ship, nearly all the crowd left us, and there remained only about twelve or thirteen passengers.

It was most amusing to watch the Frenchmen taking leave of each other, there was such a quantity of flourish and holding of hands while they paid parting compliments; besides so much bowing and taking off hats as they descended the gangway. Some of them stumbled and almost fell into the water, in their efforts to make their parting *spirituel*.

The flush deck of our steamer was of course covered with double awnings, and as the thermometer registered 86° in the shade, we rejoiced beneath punkahs in the saloon. The sea remained quite calm, while a feeble sun was shining through the damp and hazy atmosphere, and the air seemed heavy with moisture. The sheets of our beds were sticky and wet, and in the mornings we put on limp damp clothes— the result being that I contracted such a snivelling cold that I became hateful to those who dwelt alongside me.

Besides the French, we had aboard the boat five or six Englishmen and a crowd of Spaniards from Manilla. I am afraid that we shunned these Manilla men as a mosquito shuns the smoke, or as a Yankee shuns a Chinaman in California—not because they took the white man's money, as the Chinaman was supposed to do over there, but English folks always will be ridiculously British wherever they are, and we were merely an ordinary British crowd.

On the evening of June 27, the sun made but a feeble atttempt to come out, and the sea was quite rough. A feeling of nausea crept over me. I regret to have to mention it, but I became sick. I was very ill. Then I became worse. I spent the night amid basins and broken glasses in a state of moaning despondency and abject misery. Early in the morning the sea became calmer; so did I. Then I called the *garçon*, who brought me a bottle of sweet champagne, after which I was more hopeful, and absorbed the greater part of its contents with tears of gratitude in my eyes. The sea quieted down very much as the morning wore on, but as I was quite hollow I did not dare indulge in a bath; therefore my washing and dressing were almost as simple as the pirate's toilet—viz., two stamps and a damn.

I stayed on deck all day, and amused myself in watching some Malay men whom we had on board. There were about two hundred of them, all making a pilgrimage to Mecca. They were deck passengers, and lived altogether forward on one of the hatches. I daresay this was very pleasant during the midsummer weather we were suffering from.

Each of these men had one mat on which he sat, and another that he produced at sunset to perform his devotions on. This latter was much smarter, and might be termed a 'go-to-meeting' mat. They spread them out on the deck every evening, apparently at the setting of the sun, and all went through the most elaborate salaaming. There was a head pilgrim with them, who seemed to be a sort of people's caterer or guide. He had a map of the world, which he consulted at sundown, and told the others exactly whereabouts Mecca lay, so that they might turn their faces in that direction for the evening prayer.

One evening in the Red Sea he consulted his map, and appeared doubtful and uncertain. However, the hour of prayer was at hand, so he fixed his point somewhere on the starboard bow, and all the pilgrims knelt, except the *personal conductor*, who still studied his map doubtfully. Eventually he concluded that he had made a mistake, as we were passing Mecca at the time, and when the pilgrims had all finished their elaborate prayers, the conductor fixed another spot on the starboard quarter, and they all had to go through the whole of their tedious devotions again.

After leaving Singapore, our next calling place was Ceylon, where a man whom we will call 'Crab' joined us. He was one of those pale-faced fellows who live in the low country, and had a dried-up, washed-out sort of expression. Crab was not a remarkably handsome man, although he wore a long, dark-coloured beard and was blessed with a sallow complexion. There seemed to be a 'leer' always lurking on his countenance. He was what they call in story-books 'my pet aversion,' and my dislike was returned, as he hated me with a death-like hatred. He talked the whole day through, never ceasing to tell exaggerated stories of himself, his own doings and prowess, or to speak highly of his own virtues and wealth. He never swore or used bad language, but he snuffled with his nose horridly at intervals, and always told lies without faltering.

This man would not have been so objectionable if he had only kept out of one's way when he was not wanted, but he was constantly intruding himself on one unabashed. Crab could not take a snub, and always thought his company was acceptable. I was never free from that odious snuffle: wherever I went I could not get out of the reach of Crab's voice, and knowing that I was a very British Englishman, he continually worried me with the charms of a tropical life.

Crab did not smoke, and never came into the smoking-room, but he constantly stood outside the door and very often gave us the benefit of his lies while leaning against the lintel.

One day Crab was on deck, and a little Japanese came up smoking; we all smoked there, although it was done on sufferance, as the ladies could object if they wished.

Crab thought himself alone with this Japanese, and did not know how near I and one of the officers were. Then he said, 'That cigar of yours makes me faint, so take it out of your mouth,' which the Japanese refused to do, so Crab said, 'Very well, you little reptile, then I'll throw you overboard,' and advanced to do it. When he had caught hold of him, the first officer, who was standing by my side, interfered, but for some days after that they had to be kept apart, as the Japanese was a man of gentle blood, being related, as I was told, to the Princes of Satsuma, and therefore could not brook being abused without a cause. He looked anything but pleasant when we separated them, but like the Japanese, did not say anything, but only thought the more.

We scarcely had any motion worth speaking about the whole way home, except just at the beginning of the voyage, and again when we were nearing Aden, before we got into the gulf. It is true that one night a fellow who was lying asleep on one of the narrow sofas at the side of the saloon got rolled off, and did not thoroughly awaken till he found himself under the table.

This incident reminded me of an occasion when I was crossing the Pacific some years ago. Our ship, the 'Oceanic,' was rolling furiously, as a heavy wind was blowing from the southward, which came right across us. We set two jibs to steady her, but each one was immediately carried away by the force of the storm. The sea kept breaking over the decks, and one large wave came down the companion stairs and into the saloon, so that with this great wave swirling about there was scarcely any room left for us. We feared lest the whole Pacific Ocean should push its way in through the saloon doors, when the ship would be left high and dry at the bottom of the sea. All the deck and passages to our cabins were swamped, and the carpets and footstools were ruined by the inundations. After this everything was battened down tightly and all ventilation stopped, and it became terribly hot and stuffy. Sleeping in such an atmosphere and under these circumstances was like passing the night in an underground music-hall, while the noise gave it a flavour of the last day, going on all round outside. It was really dreadfully close, and we felt as poor Jonah must have felt, when he was in the whale's belly, long, long ago.

Next morning there was no cessation to our miseries. We had to hold on all the time, and we cussed each wave as it threw us on to the floor and mixed us up with the stray furniture that was sliding about.

The saloon on this ship was a particularly broad one, so that, when you slipped off the couch on which you were sitting at one side, there was a long way to go, and your body gained considerable impetus before reaching the further side. Suddenly you felt yourself going, and grabbed at anything—say, the velvet seat of the sofa on which you had been reclining—this gave way and you went sliding over the floor, velvet seat and all. In passing a chair you made a clutch at it, and it gave way also, so you all slid on together till presently you came bump up against the opposite side of the ship, which stopped you rather too abruptly.

Then, if you were not killed by the concussion, you began to collect yourself, to unravel your limbs which were entangled in the chair and cushion, your companions in adversity. But by this time the ship was rolling back again, and you found yourself at the top of a steep incline—say an angle of forty-five—with nothing firm but the floor to hold on to, so that you were obliged to slide away. Thus a perpetual racket was kept up, and you were continually rattled against the sides of the ship, like a pea in a box. However, that day the wind ceased to blow, and although we remained shut down we were able to enjoy a peaceful night, and rested without air.

CHAPTER XXX

ABOARD A M. M. STEAMER

We had an American gentleman aboard whom I will call 'The Major,' as fellows do not seem to like having their names published to the world. He was a very good fellow, except when, at the end of our voyage, he came into collision with French Government rules, and then for a time he was not pleasant; but more of this anon.

As this was a French ship, of course everyone spoke the French language aboard. It seemed that it was with difficulty at times that the Major made himself understood, in spite of (as he told me) his perfect knowledge of this tongue. He said to me one day, in confidence, 'I am almost sorry that I wasted so many of my youthful hours making myself master of a language which is so obscure that even the Frenchmen themselves cannot comprehend the meaning of much that is said to them in their own tongue.' I suggested that his Yankee accent might be at fault, but he would not allow this, as he said, 'I can write every word without a fault.' This last remark concluded the matter, and I had no further suggestions to make.

The Major was a Dutchman by birth, but in his

early boyhood he ran away to America, where he was a farmer for many years in the Western States. He found out that I also had visited the glorious West, and became very keen on talking over the old times and country with me. The first night that he made this discovery he kept me up quite late—I think it was till eleven o'clock—chatting about America, cussing all Easterners, and extolling the virtues of all Westerners, especially himself. He became quite enthusiastic about it, and I think fancied himself in the prairies again. He reproduced from the back of his memory a few of the old lies he used to tell stra*i*ngers, when he was a free American; lies which he never has the satisfaction of uttering now, for he has changed his abode to the sedate and English East.

He fought on the Republican side during the war. I somehow fancied that he was *not* one of those who occupied a position to lead on the Northern hosts to death or victory, but that is such a trifle, as *he* was under the impression that he was entitled to call himself Major, as that brought back in spirit all the glorious pageant of war. He had his letters addressed to him 'Major,' so that settled the matter.

After a bit I found the Major had still some land in Western America, which I fancied he would be willing to sell. He wanted to take *me* out to America and sell it to *me*; in fact, the old gentleman had taken quite a fancy to me, and wanted to 'do' me in all sorts of ways. He had a daughter in Switzerland whom I thought that he wanted me to marry, and one night after a good dinner he sat up on deck jödling to me like a Swiss peasant. Also he gave way to a few Yankee religious songs. I hoped, if I was made to indulge in wedlock with the Miss 'Major,' that she would not be quite so short and fat as her sire, and would not have such an exceedingly quavering voice when she accommodated me with a little religious music. Well, anyway, this Major was a capital companion aboard ship.

Sunday on a Messageries Maritimes ship is not any worse than other days, for the simple reason that one does not pay the very slightest attention to it. I really think this is rather a disadvantage, as I am an Englishman, and therefore have a lingering inclination towards church-going and different clothes on a Sunday; but it seems that in all the world it is only we Englishmen who are supplied with this hankering, and the longer one is away from home the more it is beaten out of one's constitution.

I will give you a fragment copied from my journal, *apropos* of the Sabbath Day:—'The passengers are lolling about smoking, apparently with nothing much to do. Our Ceylon friend is snuffling quite gently as though he felt the influence of Sunday, while others are reading novels and wishing for dinner-time.

'We do not play cards on Sunday; why we restrain ourselves I cannot imagine, as man is very vile on this side of the globe, and he generally sets aside the Sabbath for the working of every conceivable evil. On board ship there is scarcely room for going to and fro on the earth, and walking up and down it, as Satan used to do when he was dull; and it is the more to our credit that we abstain from cards, as there is little else to occupy us. Other days of the week we played cards every evening, and it was quite giddifying (new word introduced because it seems to fit) to watch an old French lady, who could not speak a word of our tongue, play whist every night with three Englishmen who were unable to speak French. She understood that she was to be paid when she won, but they could not prevail on her to comprehend that she ought to shell out when she lost.'

A KATAMARANG AT MOUNT LAVINIA

I forgot to say that the Major had done the right thing for such a protracted delay as this voyage seemed to be, as he came aboard with the fixed determination of reading through the whole of George Eliot's novels without missing a word. So he laid in the lot before leaving Hong Kong. If you visited his cabin at any time during the day—it mattered not if it was Sunday or weekday—he was generally to be found there in a hopeless condition of perusal. His floor was covered with volumes already digested, while on the upper berth, the 'Mill on the Floss' might be seen loitering there, in company with the third volume of 'Middlemarch.' All the rest of George Eliot's novels were somewhere about the cabin, so that, when a sea got up, I should imagine there must have been a terrible scene of wreckage. Even when the ship kept up her monotonous roll from side to side, the bindings were in terrible jeopardy.

Leaving Aden we were encouraged by the following facts. There was a ship at anchor in the harbour which had come in the day before our arrival. She had not been properly provided for a tropical voyage at this season of the year, and out of twenty-five passengers whom she had on board, seven had died of suffocation coming down the Red Sea; but they had been steaming down wind, and we were going against it. However, it was oppressively hot even for us, as the thermometer did not register below 104° for three days, the air was laden with sand from the desert, and life was almost unbearable. We passed our existence crowded together on the upper deck, sleeping and quarrelling, as, with the temperature so high, we all hated one another, and no one seemed inclined even to read.

I have got in my journal a short paragraph about one of these days—a very expressive paragraph, because there is nothing else written down on that page to mar its description—viz., 'July 10. We all hate each other aboard this ship. Thermometer 104°.'

That is what I call putting an enormous amount of meaning in a very few words.

On another page this is written: 'July 11, 12, 13, and 14. Things are going on much the same as usual. Awful heat! Damp! Punkahs! Perspiration and Tobacco!' You see we were having an intellectual time.

When we arrived at Suez, our anchor was dropped in the gulf, about two miles off the entrance to the Canal. We waited there till a steam launch came out bearing the terrible news that we were to be in quarantine, and not to enter the Canal until we had absolution telegraphed to us from certain officials in Alexandria. We were put in quarantine because the French mail had touched at Saigon, before I got aboard her in Singapore. Since her departure cases of cholera had broken out in Saigon, and it had been telegraphed home to quarantine us to prevent possible infection.

All the next day it was undecided how long we should be kept in Coventry, and we were constantly on the look-out, both with field glasses and the naked eye, to see a boat coming from the distant town bringing us tidings of our fate. Boats kept leaving shore, but they did not approach our ship, till at length the western sun sank to rest behind the yellow sand-hills which fringed that deep blue sea, and still we were left in vague uncertainty as to what our fate would be. At last, just as it was getting dark, a boat with the Government flag put off and made straight for us. She brought a telegram saying that we were only sentenced to thirty-six hours' confinement, provided the doctor whom they had brought with them could give us a clean bill of health. Then we got that doctor aboard, and he sniffed round the saloon, went into some of the cabins, and after drinking some champagne, felt equal to signing the bill of health, so that the following morning we steamed ahead again through the Suez Canal.

Coming through the Red Sea, we had had a very hot time, as the chief engineer registered 93° of heat in the water, three feet beneath the bottom of the ship, at four o'clock in the morning. Under these circumstances a bath was a hot bath: such a thing as a cold bath could not be obtained.

We passed slowly through the Canal, and encountered a good many camels being ridden by picturesquely attired natives, while other camels in long strings were carrying loads on their backs. The natives of Egypt seem to dress very much for effect, but on approaching them nearer you see how dirty they really are. The sky is beautifully blue, and the sands are dazzlingly yellow, but when you land at Port Said you find it a wretched little sink of iniquity, surrounded on three sides by yellow desert, and full of scoundrels of every nation, where it is difficult in these days even to buy a good cigarette. Fortunately, we only halted there for about eight hours, and then got into the Mediterranean.

I must refer to that man Crab again, as he declared so continually that there was no place in the world equal to his adopted island for climate, scenery, or anything else, that we at length became thoroughly tired of 'Ceylon's spicy breezes,' and only longed for 'Afric's coral strand;' for whenever you started a subject of conversation with your neighbour at table, he immediately jumped down your throat with the superiority of Ceylon. We could not make out why he was leaving an island home which he thought such perfection.

However, after a while I saw that he was getting 'dried up,' for he did not talk nearly so much, but seemed to dislike me more and more. When I was talking to my neighbours at table, he just looked on with a critical eye, every now and then coughing quietly, or shifting in his seat by way of showing that he disapproved of my statements, but did not care to contradict them.

When we had been aboard the ship for about eighteen days, I regret to say that I 'had words' with Crab; which only shows how irritable it is possible to get when bored to death on a long voyage. At breakfast one morning the *garçon* was handing some boiled eggs, when Crab remarked to himself, 'Let's see, shall I have a boiled egg or not?' After watching his indecision for a moment, I said, 'Oh yes, have an egg—it will do you good.' Upon which he arose and said in a loud voice, 'No one aboard this ship dictates to me what I shall eat or drink.' Then he retired into his deck-chair, and remained lost in his own reflections for the rest of the day.

On another occasion, I came down to breakfast and said, 'It's a fine day, the wind's fair, and I am going to have my hair cut ready for getting into port.' So Crab said, 'Who is going to cut *your* hair?' I replied, 'Why, the steward tells me that you often cut the passengers' hair, and I was going to ask if you had any objection to trying on me.' Upon which he turned very pale, and getting up from his chair, replied with the utmost dignity, 'Sir, it is evident that you have forgotten your position on this ship and mine.' Then snuffling quite loudly, he left the table, having only just begun his breakfast, and did not speak to me again for three days.

CHAPTER XXXI

WE ARRIVE AT MARSEILLES

THERE was a beautifully airy smoking-room on deck beneath the awning, where punkahs were continually pulled by Chinamen; here four Englishmen were often to be found playing whist. The Major sometimes took a hand when no one else could be found. If you could get him into the mood, he was a great hand at telling stories. He annoyed some of us by interrupting a game for the sake of an anecdote. I think I must interrupt my readers in the same way by repeating one of the Major's own.

It seems that a rather cheeky young gentleman was staying at the same hotel as the Major, and making a mistake, he bounced into the commercial room one day, whistling as he went. One of the gentlemen of commerce there first looked him all over, and then said, being rather affronted at his casual entrance, 'Are you aware, sir, that this is the commercial room?' The intruder therefore stopped his whistling, sniffed several times, and at length said, 'Law, so it is.' This tale, although very short, somehow tickled us a good deal.

Our ship was now filled with discord, and somehow our passengers were divided amongst themselves. Many of them were invalids, and consequently rather irritable and peevish, while others were naturally ill-tempered. We relieved the pitiless hours of daily sunshine with a continual 'divertissement' as to whether we should leave the ship at Naples, where we knew that there would be no quarantine, or go on to Marseilles, where the captain told us that *perhaps* we should get quarantined for a week. This remained an open question for some time, till one morning we woke up to find ourselves just entering the Straits of Messina, with Mount Etna on our left hand, and the toe of Italy on our right.

The morning was beautifully clear and calm, and in that wonderful scenery it was like passing through a bit of fairyland. At midnight we dropped anchor off Naples, where we were only to remain a couple of hours. All the lights in our cabins had been put out an hour before, and the *maître d'hôtel* refused to light them again. This was before electricity had become an established thing on board the Messageries boats. Thereupon the most awful confusion ensued that one can possibly imagine, as many of the passengers had to pack up their things in the dark, and get off the ship in little open boats; whilst, to add to their difficulties, the most horrible thunderstorm was now raging, and the rain kept pouring down in torrents.

These difficulties were much more than I cared to contend with, and I remained aboard watching the struggles of my three English friends, and Crab, who, I am delighted to say, left us at Naples.

By half-past two the rain had ceased, the anchor had been weighed, we were off again, and quiet being once more restored, I slunk away to bed.

Towards noon on the following day, we saw a faint

outline of coast as we were now off Toulon. The weather had become quite cool and pleasant again, and the day was remarkably fine with a civilised haze over the distance, such as we had not seen for many a month.

At about four o'clock we found ourselves pretty close to the coast, and as we hoped to get to Marseilles before dark, everyone was on the look out for the longed-for home. Even the Major left an unfinished proposal of George Eliot's in his cabin to come and see the promised land. It was worth looking at, as the day being fine and the sea calm, the hilly coast-line stood out very prettily. White sails were scattered over the distant waters, and birds came floating behind the vessel once more. A certain change was visible over the whole ship, and the placid routine of every-day life appeared to be interrupted, as sailors kept coming aft to undo ropes and arrange chains.

At five o'clock we found ourselves very close to the high white cliffs. But there always seemed to be another promontory to pass before we should finally arrive alongside the shore.

At six the sky began to turn red for the approaching sunset, and a more gentle evening and perfect sunset I never saw. Everyone was collected on deck: some of our passengers had not seen European lands for eight or nine years, while others were invalids who longed for their home and rest.

At last we came very suddenly round a projecting headland on to Marseilles, and the clean looking European town with its white houses. The distant roar of the carts and carriages along the streets were sweet sounds to us homeward bound. All on deck gave way to one cheer of delight as their long-wished-for haven came in sight.

We talked of what we should do when we landed, where we should dine and sleep. Most of the passengers had put on their shore clothes and packed up their things ready for a start.

We glided slowly into port, and there came out in boats healthy-looking European men, sunburnt sailors, women in holiday dresses, friends, wives and children to greet some of the passengers. But they did not come aboard. . . .

They could not come aboard . . . for there also came out to the ship's side a small boat carrying a yellow flag, which stopped those who wished to board us, and brought the fatal news that we must first endure five days at least of quarantine before we might set foot upon that glittering shore.

This was a terrible blow.

We had to turn sadly round and steam out of port, to steam away across the bay to a desolate spot called the Quarantine Harbour, where we went to bed mourning, and thinking sadly of the beautiful France on which we had in anticipation already landed.

How odious the ship and fellow passengers seemed next morning, and how we cursed our luck and imprisonment! We found ourselves in a small basin enclosed on all sides by high limestone rocks, so that we could not even behold the open sea from our place of anchorage.

We were not allowed to leave the ship, except to touch the nearest shore, and walk up and down a few hundred yards of bare white road, the connecting link between two islands. This road had an armed sentry at either end, to prevent our straying beyond the narrow prescribed limits. That was a sun-scorched, dreary time. The rays of the sun beat down on us from a cloudless sky, and the earth all round the harbour was treeless, yellow, and rock-bound. There was nothing to disturb the calmness of our weary waiting days. We thought of the people ashore enjoying this lovely weather, while we were being baked to death in this most dreary spot.

After a couple of days I found the way to enjoy a bathe in the sea, which was by landing on this piece of artificial road, and cajoling the sentinels to let me climb over the wall behind it, where I could undress and bathe on the further side without being seen. The water was deliciously cool, and wonderfully transparent, with the bottom so covered with sea-urchins that I was afraid to rest in my swim for fear of their poisonous prickles.

One day an old fisherman came along collecting sea-urchins, and taught us the way to eat them. First you get a long pole with a three-spiked prong at the end, with which you dig them off the rocks beneath the water; then you scoop out the fish with a dirty pocket-knife, and spread the roe which is found adhering to the top of the shell on a split roll covered with butter, which you have brought concealed in your pocket. Sea-urchins are a very good form of food for folks in quarantine, living on two meals only at ten francs a day.

It is curious how the worst side of human nature shows itself when one is in confinement. We seemed so tired of one another's society, and so annoyed at being imprisoned through no fault of our own, that the greatest ill-temper was shown between the passengers on all occasions. The Major was the only English-speaking friend I had left, but he was rather deaf, and so much occupied with his wrongs that I tried to avoid him, as he talked of nothing but his detention, and having to pay ten francs a day out of his own pocket for his board. He continually paced the deck with clenched fists, swearing that he would not pay a penny of it, but would compel the wretched French Government, not only to pay for his keep, but also damages for his loss of valuable time.

He was going to write a statement of his case to the 'New York Herald,' and let all America know what he was suffering at the hands of the miserable Frenchmen. In fact, there seemed little doubt that he would make a stir in the world on his arrival in the lands of civilisation. However, I never heard any talk about it afterwards. Doubtless the 'New York Herald' thought it would be a pity to subvert all our rules of civilisation by putting in an article against an institution which is carried out by all the ruling powers in this world. Or perhaps the Major thought better of his resolution when he got ashore, and tore up all his threats against the French Government; anyway, I believe that it fell through.

At this juncture, the Major had a lot of George Eliot's novels for sale *very* cheap.

There was another small steamer and a sailing vessel, who were our companions in quarantine. We watched with the most exceeding interest, through telescopes, every movement that took place on these ships. Those aboard seemed to have absolutely nothing to wile away the tedious hours of sunlight, except to stare back at us. Imagine, therefore, the situation of two steamers lying alongside one another just far enough off to make it worth while studying each other through glasses; a row of quarantine passengers on each ship, only wishing that something might happen aboard the other worth looking at. But nothing came of it, and when we had spent five days in this profitless way, at eleven o'clock one morning we weighed anchor, and steaming across the few miles of sea that separated us from Marseilles, by exactly twelve o'clock we were *free*.

The Major now entertained me at a breakfast in one of the restaurants, where we enjoyed the fruits of the earth without regard to our digestions. When he had drowned his spleen in champagne, he became the gay Yankee once more. It was a lovely day, and we sauntered about all the afternoon enjoying everything—the shops, the crowds of people, and the sea as seen from the land. Every woman looked pretty, and every man benign. Our twenty-five centimes 'Londres' seemed perfection, and life was once more full of hope.

At six we dined beneath the shadow of trees near the station, and smoked afterwards in some neatly kept gardens near the terminus, where the Major indulged once again in the songs of his Fatherland, and I was quite sorry when at nine o'clock I had to leave him and shake his hand at parting.

Two days later I arrived in London, where I bought a new hat and some tobacco.

These things were necessary, as the hat I had on had been purchased at the bazaars in Colombo, many a weary month before, and was not quite in the fashion.

Will my readers just peep at me once more?

It is six o'clock in the evening. An English lady and two girls were sitting under an aged oak-tree by the wooden gate which leads into the lane at my home in Wiltshire. They were having afternoon tea in company with three dogs. They had had the tea-table put well under the shade, as the weather was remarkably hot and fine that summer afternoon. The world was green, bright, and still all round them, and the distant downs, which you could see through a clump of red-barked Scotch firs, were almost hidden in a blue summer haze. The waters of the little lake below were quite still, except for the occasional swirl of a mighty moving pike, and all Nature seemed to rest in the July hush. The great trees near the lake seemed to peep sleepily down into the gentle, weed-grown waters, and far, far above were swallows sweeping round in distant ovals against the deep-blue English sky.

A one-horse fly was coming up the drive, and in it a weary traveller, sick of travelling, was coming to rest in the peaceful oasis of an English home.

APPENDIX

A FEW FACTS ABOUT CEYLON, LABUAN, NORTH BORNEO, AND BRUNEI

THE island of Labuan has been a British colony since 1847.

The British North Borneo Company was formed in 1882. It took over all rights, territorial and sovereign, from the Sultans of Brunei and Sulu; the protocol being signed in 1885.

Galle, in Ceylon, has infinitely the most equable temperature out of fifty-one stations given by Blanford in his 'Practical Guide to the Climates and Weather of India, Ceylon, and Burmah, in 1889.' Colombo, being so near Galle, is not given in this work, but Cochin, in the Madras Presidency, with a range of 28°, is the next nearest. The temperature of Galle is, at its highest, 89°, and at its lowest, 70°; being only an annual range of 19°.

The first time that I came to Ceylon I brought with me from England a barometer, which proved utterly useless, as the change of readings in the hills of Ceylon seems to be less than a tenth of an inch in the year. I believe that a real change only occurs once a year, at the bursting of the south-west monsoon.

The average rainfall at Colombo is 87·3 inches, and at Galle 90·7. The rainfall on the western slopes of mountains in the interior of the island, where the south-west monsoon is felt, is considerably over this. In many parts—take, for instance, Ambegamona—it is *double* that of Galle.

The equable temperature and the high rainfall make Ceylon peculiarly adapted for tea-growing.

NORTH BORNEO

The following are some extracts from the 'Handbook of British North Borneo,' which, I believe, was compiled by the North Borneo Government for perusal *in England* :—

'The area acquired by the British North Borneo Company is some 80,000 square miles in extent, and forms a sort of irregular triangle, more than two-thirds of which are bounded by the sea. The coast extends over 600 miles, and all islands within three leagues were included in the cession.

'North Borneo has the advantage of being out of the region of typhoons' (now draw in your breath). 'Earthquakes and volcanoes—which periodically work such havoc and ruin in the Spanish settlements of the Philippines in the north, and the Dutch possessions of Java and Sumatra further south—are unknown there.'

Although the tobacco estates of British North Borneo are not at present the most healthy localities that I have visited, still, when the land round Deli in Sumatra was first opened, it was equally injurious to the health of both the Chinese and Europeans. This must be the case in all low-lying districts in the tropics, which are grown over by swampy jungle, and where good water is unobtainable. Until European influence has let fresh air into these scenes of fœtid distemper, and introduced artesian wells, or other means of obtaining wholesome water, it must remain so unhealthy that Europeans cannot exist there, and even the natives only live in a few houses along the tidal rivers' banks.

There seems little doubt that the tobacco estates will eventually pay well, although, from what I can learn, the soil is quite different to the flat lands of Sumatra, which are formed from the deposit coming off volcanic mountains, whereas these Bornean flats were formed by the wash from Tertiary mountains.

'*Tobacco.*—About nineteen years ago it was discovered that tobacco grown in certain parts of the East Indian Archipelago was particularly adapted for use as wrappers for cigars; and Deli, North Sumatra, soon attracted capital and labour, until the importation into Amsterdam and Rotterdam of East Indian tobacco increased from thirty thousand pounds in 1865 to seventeen million pounds in 1882, and has since been steadily increasing.

'Many fortunes were made in Sumatra by private individuals, and several large companies sprang into existence, which have continued to flourish, many having paid dividends of *over* 100 per cent.

'Planters in Deli are hampered by heavy taxation, and, as suitable land is now difficult to obtain, a new field is eagerly sought by tobacco planters. The first Deli planter who explored the territory of the British North Borneo Company wrote:—" The first tobacco leaves were brought to me at Niow, on a very steep high hill, and when I saw the character of the plant, though only in a few poor leaves, culled and brought to me by a native, I was amply rewarded, and knew from that moment that North Borneo would be a tobacco-producing country."

'Tobacco of an excellent quality has long been known to exist in North Borneo. The soil, with its covering of "humus," is very suitable, and the seasons are favourable. Planting takes place in April or May, and in seventy days the leaves are gathered, so that three months only elapse from the time the seeds are put in the nursery beds until the gathering of the harvest.'

I think that some Bornean cigars which we obtained in

Sandakan burnt a whiter ash than any cigars I have ever seen. These cigars had been made up in Holland with Bornean tobacco for the outside wrapper, but of what leaves the interiors were composed I do not know.

I will also insert here a few paragraphs about swamp produce, copied from the same book.

SWAMP PRODUCE

'The greater part of the coast is lined to a considerable depth with enormous mangrove and nipa swamps. One alone of these swamps, extending eastwards from Sandakan Bay for sixty or seventy miles, with an average depth of ten miles or so, contains some four hundred thousand acres. This great acreage of apparently useless swamp is, however, likely to be a source of great wealth in the future. These swamps are everywhere traversable by numerous lagoons, backwaters, and creeks.

'*Mangrove* grows on what is really shallow sea, and mangrove swamps should not be, and in fact frequently are not, marked on the map as other than sea. Mangrove wood is much used as fuel, and even after paying a small freight to Hong Kong, is bought there by some people in preference to coal.

'*Mangrove Bark* is used as a dye and also for tanning purposes. Analysis has shown that it contains 41·398 per cent. of tannic acid.

'It is a well-known fact that by doing away with mangrove swamps much sickness is caused; but, in addition to the distance they are from any of our towns, their size is such that they will meet the largest requirements ever likely to be made upon them without showing any perceptible diminution.

'*Nipa Palms.*—Above the mangrove, and where the water begins to be brackish, nipa palms commence, and large swamps of them intervene between the mangroves and the true land. Those nearer the sea are comparatively small and stunted; but where the water is more fresh than salt, the leaves attain a height of twenty feet and upwards, presenting a very handsome appearance, resembling the single fronds of a huge fern. This graceful palm is utilised in various ways, the principal being in the manufacture of thatching for house-roofs, in Borneo called attaps. This manufacture is quite an industry of itself, and affords employment to many natives, chiefly women, the men simply bringing cargoes of the fronds to the women, to be stitched with split rattans and made up.

'Attap roofs are the best adapted for the Borneo climate, for, whilst the winds are never strong enough to blow them away, they afford the coolest protection against the sun of any kind of roofing known. Attaps are being shipped to China, and, if they gain in favour, there are the possibilities of a very large trade being established.

'Kadjan mats, also manufactured out of nipa leaves, are indispensable for travelling purposes; packed up in the smallest compass when not required, each one is capable of affording sufficient accommodation at night for two or three people, either in boat or forest journeys. They also almost exclusively form the material for side walls and divisions within houses.

'The young nipa leaf, unfolded and dried, forms the favourite covering for cigarettes amongst the natives. The fruit is eaten, and, indeed, on one occasion in the old days, when Sandakan ran out of rice, the people had nothing else to live upon for a whole month. In taste and appearance it is something like a cocoanut, but much tougher. In Sulu, salt—and, somewhat strange to say, sugar also—is made from the burnt stem of this palm; considerable quantities of this salt are imported into Sandakan, where the people have not yet cared to make it for themselves.

'*Nebong Palms.*—Above the nipa, and where the water

is almost fresh, the nebong grows. It is plentiful in low and somewhat swampy places along the coast, and is generally a sign of the presence of fresh water in the vicinity. It attains a height of forty to fifty feet. The unsplit round trunks are used for the posts of Malay houses, while when split up they are employed for flooring, rafters, &c. As a rule, the posts do not last more than three or four years, but as the wood is plentiful, and requires no preliminary preparation beyond cutting to the proper lengths, this disadvantage is the less felt. The head, or cabbage, formed of the unexpanded leaves, is a delicious vegetable.

'Its utility to the natives will be understood from the fact that nearly all the houses in the city of Brunei, with a population reckoned at 20,000, as well as the rough bridges, or "jumbatans," connecting them, are built of this palm over the water of the river of that name. This tree will be found most useful by tobacco-planters for all temporary buildings, such as drying-houses, coolie-lines, and so forth, and some have been already exported to Sulu for these purposes.'

This is a fragment from the 'Brunei Directory,' which consists of five pages only:

'When the Spaniards first became acquainted with Brunei, a state of things existed in the capital greatly different and superior to what they are in our time. Then a royal audience was conducted with great pomp and splendour; now it is an empty form. Then courtiers were clothed in silk; now they strut about in the filthiest homespun, and are of the venal description. It seems only a matter of time when Brunei as an independent state shall, from sheer inertia, cease to exist.'

I cull these morsels from the same:

Under the heading of Marine Department one ship only is given.

Steam Launch 'Enterprise.'

Captain	Kassim.
Engineer	Sarail.

Her Britannic Majesty's Consulate.

Agent at Brunei	Inchi Mahomet.
Carpenters	Ah Wah.

Mr. Ah Wah ought to be a proud man, and I hope that he thinks a lot of himself, as in this directory he was put down as what might be a crowd of carpenters.

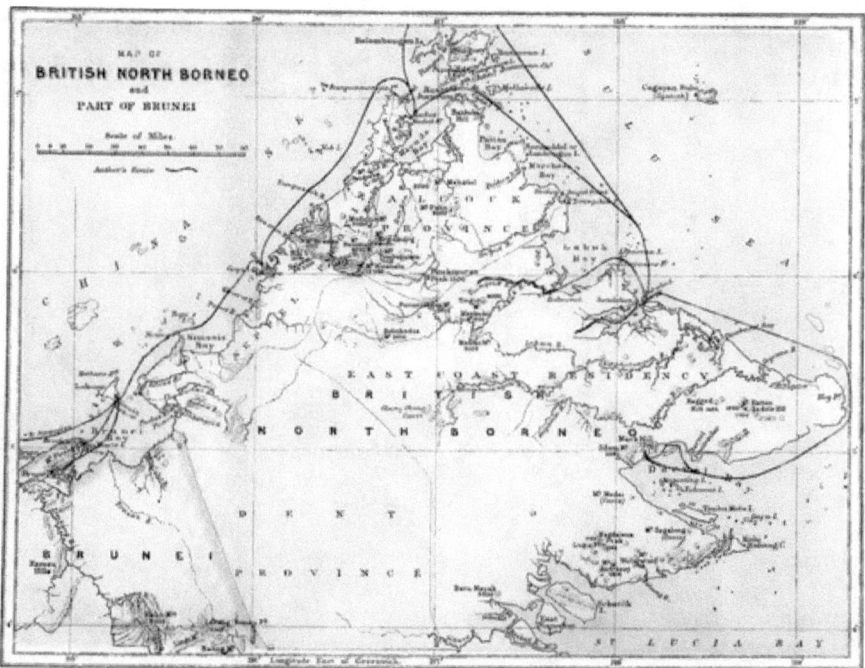

www.ingramcontent.com/pod-product-compliance
Lightning Source LLC
Chambersburg PA
CBHW032054230426
43672CB00009B/1593